A MILLIONAIRE'S CLOUT!

We all know the bad news: Inflation is devouring our savings.

But now at last there's good news: We all can actually profit from inflation.

The same inflation that has pushed up prices has also skyrocketed interest rates paid to those who put their money in the right places. Previously, only the very rich could take advantage of this situation to make a virtually risk-free financial killing. But now high-yielding money market funds and other attractive financial instruments let the average person share in this wealth of opportunity to make money multiply.

You no longer need a big bankroll. All you need to find and make the best deal for you and your money is enough time to read and use this book—

THE SMART INVESTOR'S GUIDE TO THE MONEY MARKET

PAUL SARNOFF is Director of Research for a leading commodity broker and has written thirty books on business and investment. He has edited several money magazines, lectured both in the United States and abroad, and managed his clients' investments in stocks, options and commodities for over forty years.

THE SMART INVESTOR'S GUIDE TO THE MONEY MARKET

by
Paul Sarnoff

A SIGNET BOOK
NEW AMERICAN LIBRARY
TIMES MIRROR

For My Beloved Mother-in-Law
Tillie Levitt

SIGNET TRADEMARK REG. U.S. PAT. OFF. AND FOREIGN COUNTRIES
REGISTERED TRADEMARK—MARCA REGISTRADA
HECHO EN CHICAGO, U.S.A.

SIGNET, SIGNET CLASSICS, MENTOR, PLUME, MERIDIAN AND NAL BOOKS are published by The New American Library, Inc., 1633 Broadway, New York, New York 10019.

First Printing, November, 1981

3 4 5 6 7 8 9

PRINTED IN THE UNITED STATES OF AMERICA

Contents

Introduction

Welcome to the money market game. It's played in a multi-billion-dollar computerized arena where leading corporations, the federal government, states, and cities come to borrow short-term funds. These funds, in turn, are supplied principally by institutional and private investors and by concentrated sources of money from commercial banks, thrift institutions (including savings banks and savings and loan associations), and money market funds (hereinafter called money funds).

In the money market game, return from high interest paid by borrowers, coupled with relatively low risk on the part of lenders, can multiply your money much faster and much more safely than at any other time in American history.

In July 1981 an innovative commercial bank advertised a 20% per year simple interest reward for deposits left for 66 months . . . thrifts advertised rates of almost 16% for federally insured 6-month $10,000 money market certificates . . . other thrifts advertised 16% for uninsured deposits of as little as $1,000 held for 7 to 77 days or 8 to 88 days . . . and many money funds aggressively advertised yields in excess of 17% (compounded daily), also uninsured.

And by August, such advertising efforts by various financial institutions were spreading through the media like prairie fires. Indeed, the dazzlingly diverse offers of money-making options available to you and to me in the summer of 1981 were not only unprecedented but almost unbelievable.

But you'd better believe it. And you'd be wise to learn how to make the smartest moves that will cause your money to grow in the money market game—with sensible safety—whether interest rates remain at current levels, decline, or go higher in the future. Your primary objective in playing this game should be to try to get the best yield possible with the least risk on your *reserve* money. By reserve money I mean funds that have to be liquid enough for you to get at quickly to pay for planned expenses like down payments on a house, or other big ticket items like the payment of taxes, purchase of investments, and college tuition payments. In other words, this is money that you want to set aside for some future purpose without entailing loss of principal, and at the same time have it work harder and earn more money for you than it normally would in a passbook savings account.

To assist you in building reserve funds, I have attempted to write this book for the *smart investor*, those of you who are interested in building up reserves with a minimum of risk. I have always believed that the most beneficial weapon for financial betterment is the intelligent application of the lessons of experience. So I hope you will use what follows to get smart and build reserves in today's weirdly high interest-rate world. If you already are a smart investor, perhaps you will become even smarter after you read—and I hope enjoy—what follows.

My definition of a smart investor:

S . . . a person who basically seeks *Safety* of principal.

M . . . a person who seeks to *Maximize Money*—with safety.

A . . . a person who seeks to *Accumulate* money for the future.

R . . . a person who is willing to *Research* the alternatives.

T . . . a person who makes *Trouble-free* decisions with cash reserves.

You should find enough in this book to help you do your own thinking when you read the startling ads offering amazingly generous yields during times when interest rates are high and short-term money is sought. You should also find the route to making money on your reserve money safely and wisely whether we continue into an era of increasing inflation or, because of governmental monetary policy, encounter deflationary recession.

Please remember: the smart investor asks questions *before* investing—not after.

1
Smart Money Basics

Safe Money Explained

In my long-standing role as a money-funnel for the Internal Revenue Service, I have been ably assisted by my wife. While I kept busy for decades handling millions upon millions of risk dollars for myself and for clients, she busied herself husbanding our *safe money*, making sure we earned the maximum available interest without *ever* endangering the principal.

I distinctly remember that on the day after our wedding in 1940, she shoved 60% of our total assets into a safe bank account in Washington, D.C. Since our cash reserve only amounted to $5—and the sole Sarnoff bank account amounted at first to $3—the rate of interest on our savings wasn't too important.

But as the years passed, our safe money began to accumulate to such an extent that my wife was able to shuffle her bankbooks around hither and yon to obtain the highest rates possible for insured savings.

Our safe savings, of course, received a tremendous boost in 1978, when commercial banks and thrifts were permitted to issue money market certificates with interest related to U.S. Treasury bill rates.

Thereafter, my wife shifted a good deal of our savings from passbook accounts to certificate accounts so we could receive about triple the yield on our safe money formerly held inside the very same banks and thrifts in a lower-yielding form—and at the same time benefit from the toasters and gifts given away by most banks and thrifts in the growing war for fresh deposits. Now we not only began to relish the double digit—and insured—interest multiplying our savings, but we were also better able to enjoy summers at the beach with the free blankets, chaises, beach chairs, totes, and transistor radios.

In April 1979 I traveled to Houston, Texas, to address the Financial Analysts Federation's annual convention on the subject of precious metals. A few weeks after my talk, I received reimbursement for travel and hotel expenses. The check was drawn by the federation treasurer on an account at the Dreyfus Liquid Assets Fund.

I naturally mentioned this to my wife and she told me that our son, an attorney who is commodity counsel for a major brokerage firm, had been twisting her arm to borrow at 1% above her passbook rate on some of her savings accounts and put the money at triple the yield in a money fund. Since we had had some ups and downs with mutual funds in the past, she was reluctant to risk our insured savings in an investment company that would not guarantee a steady rate of return—or even insure the principal. But when she saw that the Financial Analysts Federation kept a reserve account with a money fund to pay bills that ran over $500, she became really interested.

After some self-education—with my attorney son's help, of course—my wife lost some of her former timidity. At first, she made a modest investment in a money fund. Then, like so many other investors all over the country, she began to regard the dividends paid daily by her fund as "interest." And after becoming acquainted with the investment objectives and methods of portfolio management in these funds, she actually began to believe that buying money fund shares was almost as safe as making insured bank or thrift deposits.

While nothing could be further from the truth, my rather conservative spouse, who probably wouldn't ante in a stud poker game without aces back-to-back, began to maneuver our reserve money in such a manner that she now has the following "safe money" management tools:

1. One or more certificate and passbook accounts at a local thrift.
2. One or more savings and checking accounts at a local savings bank.
3. A money fund account at a large stockbrokerage house.
4. A T-bill account at a commodity broker.
5. Miscellaneous money market certificate and Treasury-bill certificate accounts at banks.
6. Miscellaneous money market certificate accounts at thrifts.

Her approach is simply to "eat her safe-money-high-interest cake—and have it."

As certificates mature, she either "rolls them over" (renews the certificates) if the yield exceeds 15%; or cashes the certificates and parks the money in her money fund, where it earns high daily compounded dividends until something better appears. Of course, as we receive fresh money from income and investments, she parks the new funds in the money fund until they have to be used to pay for big-ticket items.

The advantage of doing this is immediately obvious. If I formerly had to make a tax payment four times a year on money I hadn't earned yet and drew the funds from a bank savings account, my earned interest ended immediately with the withdrawal. Now I send the IRS a money fund check that may take ten days before it is returned to be charged to the fund account. Waiting for the check to clear is called the "float." And using a money fund check will assure me of receiving an additional ten-day dividend because of the float. Naturally I could pay the IRS with a check on my checking account and it would take about the same time to clear. But I cannot get the kind of interest on my checking account that I can earn with dividends from the money fund while waiting for the check to clear.

In fact, most people do not receive any interest from the bank on their checking account balances. So earning high-yielding dividends on the float is one of the big advantages of keeping reserve funds in a money fund instead of in a bank checking account.

My wife has come to regard her money fund as a *money management tool*, rather than as a depository. For example, on July 9, 1981, she noticed a full-page ad in *The New York Times* announcing that a savings bank in Brooklyn, New York, was offering something called "Sky-Hi Interest Account," inviting savers to "lock in" a "guaranteed rate and FDIC insured deposit for a full 48 months." The stated rate was 17.803%. My wife's first reaction was to think, "Maybe I'll lock in some money at this rate for the next four years: interest rates can't stay at this level forever."

Since her money fund account approximated six figures—without decimals—all she had to do was clip the coupon in the ad, write a check, and send it off. She didn't—but if she had sent $50,000 and the fund she would have drawn the check on paid 17.6%, she would have earned $239.40 extra during the ten-day interval when the check was floating.

In summary, the only *really safe* money is money invested either in direct obligations of the federal government, its agencies, or deposited in bank or thrift accounts that are insured by an agency of the government. Investments either in money market debt instruments that are obligations of banks or large corporations or in money funds that position such debt instruments are actually not safe, but can be classified instead as "low risk."

Low-Risk Money Explained

While stock market activity commands the lion's share of editorial attention in the financial press, 95% to 97% of all money that moves around daily in financial centers involves *debt*, not equity. This debt can be in the form of bonds (long-term obligations) issued by federal, state, and municipal bodies, and corporations—publicly or privately held. It can be in the form of notes (obligations to repay on a certain date bearing a stated amount of interest) that run for one year and up. Or the debt can be in the form of short-term promises to repay that run from one day to one year.

It is such short-term promises that represent the debt purchased by the money funds. Because these funds buy money market securities that have very brief maturities (usually less than sixty days) and are issued by the government, the largest banks, and publicly traded corporations, they are considered low-risk—and *practically* safe.

The money funds I consider practically safe will hold debt securities with the shortest maturity in times of rising interest rates and debt securities of longer maturity when interst rates are declining. If they operate in this manner, the resulting yields reported on a weekly or monthly basis stack up favorably with the average for the industry. If they don't, the performance drops below the industry average, and intelligent fundholders may liquidate and shift to a better-paying fund.

The one real danger in any money fund operation is that if the portfolio is poorly managed, a majority of the fund's holders may decide to move their money to a better-paying fund, with mass liquidation of the fund portfolio as the result. This can obviously cause liquidity problems. But chances are that the funds—which are able to borrow and can also raise cash via repurchase agreements—can come up with all the money to meet any emergency liquidation demands.

Constant $1-a-Share Value

The money funds I favor are those that maintain a constant daily $1-a-share value. In this type of fund, the daily interest earned by the fund on its investment portfolio (after deduction of expenses) is allocated and credited to each shareholder's account. Thus, if you open an account today at a money fund of this nature with $1,000, you'll purchase 1,000 shares of the fund. The next day those 1,000 shares will have earned a share in the interest received by the fund. Your reward will be expressed in added shares that will again earn something the following day, and so on. Assume at the end of the month that your "yield" has been $14 on the initial $1,000 investment; your share holding will then be 1,014. In other words, your dollar equity in the fund will be $1,014, since each share equals precisely $1.

Investments in any other kind of mutual fund represent *real risk*, not low risk, because the value of your holdings in such funds depends upon the market value of the underlying securities divided by the number of shares of the fund issued and outstanding. Thus an investment of $1,000 in a so-called "growth" fund could find your holdings at the end of a month worth $1,016, or $987, or whatever. But in a $1-constant-value-per-share money fund, your holdings are always worth $1 a share—and the growth of those dollars into more shares each day depends upon the ability of the fund advisers to make your money multiply through receipt of high money market interest, instead of attempting to build your funds via long- or short-term capital gains or trading profits.

Maximizing Reserves Safely

In introducing you to my concepts of "safe money" and "practically safe (low-risk) money," my primary purpose is to provide you with the beginnings of a reasonable road map that will lead you to strategies that will enable you to get the most return on your money with the least risk to your reserve funds.

You could invest directly in money market debt instruments—if you had the time and at least a million dollars worth of investment capital. You would also need the knowledge, expertise, and contacts to get the very best offerings available in the money market. Or you could elect to have an experienced professional adviser do this for you for a fee.

But probably the best alternative for most of us—and a convenient one at that—is to invest in money funds which in turn pool our money and invest it for us in those debt instruments.

2

Meet the Money Funds

Money Talk

In early August 1981 the hottest topic of conversation wherever you went no longer involved the sinking price of gold. What everyone seemed to be asking was, "Which money fund do you have money in, and how much 'interest' are you getting?"

All of a sudden conservative savers (small and large) woke up to realize they could earn yields of 17% or more (for seven days anyway) on amounts as little as $1,000—without penalty for early withdrawal. And with widely publicized weekly yield of money funds averaging 17%, it became obvious that investment in these low-risk media could whip inflation by a tremendous margin, especially when government statistics began to indicate that the official annual inflation rate had dropped below 10%.

To add spice to the increasingly popular topic of money funds, the daily press and periodicals such as *Money* magazine began to run articles touting them. William Donoghue, the so-called Guru of the Money Funds, had been peregrinating around the country for some time, appearing at seminars on money. Merrill Lynch began conducting seminars about money funds and how they could be used effectively to multiply money rapidly.

Money funds, of course, have been around for years,

but until recently they had always kept a relatively low advertising profile. In the summer of 1981, though, many of the funds stepped up their advertising aggressively and began to spend big money to acquaint the rather uninformed public about the money funds' banklike services.

And their success in attracting investors has been quite phenomenal. On August 4, 1981, the total assets of these giant pools of reserve monies exceeded $140 billion, considerably more than double the amount at the end of March 1980.

According to the Investment Company Institute (ICI), there were over 8 million money fund accounts by August 1981. Obviously, the money funds had to be doing something right for their risk-takers, in order to grow at such an astonishing pace in 17 months. Moreover, the assets of 26 of the 75 money funds listed in *The New York Times* (several times a week) exceeded a billion dollars each. Here are the ten largest money funds as of August 4, 1981:

Money Funds: The Top Ten (August 4, 1981)

Rank	*Money fund*	*Asset Size ($-billions)*	*7-day yield*	*30-day yield*
1.	Merrill Lynch Ready Assets Trust	$18.56	16.9%	16.6%
2.	Merrill CMA Money Trust	8.60	17.2	16.9
3.	InterCapital Liquid Asset Fund	7.83	17.5	17.1
4.	Dreyfus Liquid Assets	6.70	17.4	17.4
5.	Cash Reserve Management	5.84	17.8	17.6
6.	Paine Webber Cashfund	4.60	17.0	17.0
7.	Daily Cash Accumulation Fund	4.52	17.6	17.6
8.	Shearson Daily Dividend	4.40	17.4	17.3
9.	Fidelity Daily Income Trust	3.49	17.1	17
10.	Tempfund	3.28	17.3	17.1
	Total:	$67.82		

Whether the long-term top yield among these leading money funds will turn out to be Hutton's Cash Reserve

Management (#5 above table), or Shearson's Daily Dividend (#8), or Dean Witter's InterCapital (#3 in the table) depends directly upon the performance of each fund's investment adviser. Still, it is interesting to note that eight out of the ten largest money funds are distributed directly by stockbrokerage firms.

Brokers have never been accused of being philanthropists, so there must be sound reasons for their involvement in money funds. For that matter, insurance companies are also aggressively going after the savings of people around the country to swell the assets of the money funds that they now sponsor and distribute. Management companies of major mutual fund organizations represent the third major category of money fund backers.

What a Money Fund Is

Before belaboring the reasons why stockbrokers, insurance companies, and investment company managements are increasingly active in offering savers and investors banklike services at much better returns than the traditional passbook accounts, let's define and explore what a money fund is, and how it invests in order to throw off daily dividends from high interest received in low-risk money market investments.

Like every other investment company (mutual fund) registered under the Investment Company Act of 1940, a modern money fund offers shares to the public, invests those shares at low risk in selected short-term debt securities, and allocates the interest income to each registered shareholder, according to the number of shares in the shareholder's account.

But unlike the mutual funds that invest in shares of AT&T, General Motors, or General Electric, in order to earn both dividends and capital gains for shareholders, money funds seek to achieve high interest yields from *debt instruments* rather than stock equities. The interest earned each day by the money fund is applied in the form of new shares that earn more money each day for the shareholders. Thus, you can look at your investment in a money fund as shares that grow to more shares, or money that multiplies into more money. And the way the shares earn more money is simply that the investment adviser of the fund purchases promissory obligations that the government, big banks, and large corporations sell in the money market virtually on a daily basis to meet immediate or near-term cash needs.

Still, money funds are *not* bank or thrift account substitutes for emergency savings. They actually are *no-load* (no up-front entry charges or exit deductions) and *open-end* (new shares are issued to investors from the fund's authorized number of shares and cancelled when the investor liquidates, so that there is no fixed capitalization at any one time, and new buyers or additions to holdings by existing shareholders can be readily accommodated) mutual funds that invest *only* in selected money market debt instruments.

Just as in mutual stock funds that invest in equity securities, all money funds have three basic features:

1. A *management company* that markets (distributes) the money fund shares directly or through agents
2. An *investment adviser* who makes all the investment decisions on behalf of the fund shareholders
3. A *custodian bank* or trust company to keep the fundholders' portfolio safe and secure

An IDS Cash Management Fund advertisement succinctly explains, "A Money Market Fund operates on a simple principle: Pooling. It receives relatively small amounts of money from a large number of individuals and small businesses . . . pools that money . . . and lends it to the money market with the degree of care and expertise as would any other major lender. The interest earned is then passed along to the Fund's investors, or 'shareholders,' as dividends. Therefore, you as a shareholder would have the advantage of earning 'money market' interest."

Money Market Interest

Because the borrowers in the modern money market require huge sums of money for very brief periods and because most of the money market debt instruments are unsecured, the borrowers generally will pay much higher interest rates than if the debt were collateralized by property, securities, or other tangibles. (Chapter 3 explains the types of money market debt securities bought and redeemed by money funds.)

Obviously these debt instruments—which are available in the new issue market and in the secondary (resale) securities market mainly to industrial, institutional, and financial corporations seeking to use spare cash flow intelligently—involve millions upon millions of debt-dollars. Thus, the best opportunities in this highly professional market are not readily available to private investors with less than a million dollars to lend.

But the money fund innovators realized that while people might balk at making risk investments entailing gain or loss, they could hardly object to *lending* their money at high interest if that money were *professionally pooled and managed.* Thus, money funds today throw off almost as good a yield to an investor with $1,000 as someone could win in the money market game with as much as a million dollars to invest.

It logically follows that if you invest in any of the 23 money funds open to private investors whose assets exceed a billion dollars, you will give your investment a billionaire's clout in the money market.

Here is a list of such funds as of August 4, 1981:

Money Funds with Billionaire's Clout

*Fund Size (in $-billions)**	*Fund Name*	*7-day yield*	*30-day yield*
$1.55	Alliance Capital Reserves	17.1%	17.0%
1.22	Capital Preservation Fund II	15.7	16.5
2.78	Cash Equivalent Fund	17.8	17.7
5.84	Cash Reserve Management	17.8	17.7
1.20	Current Interest	17.2	17.2
4.53	Daily Cash Accumulation Fund	17.6	17.6
6.70	Dreyfus Liquid Assets	17.4	17.4
2.45	Fidelity Cash Reserves	17.2	17.2
3.49	Fidelity Daily Income Trust	17.1	17.0
7.83	InterCapital Liquid Asset Fund	17.5	17.1
2.26	Kemper Money Market Fund	17.9	17.6
1.84	Liquid Capital Income	17.5	17.3
8.60	Merrill CMA Money Trust	17.2	17.2
18.56	Merrill Lynch Ready Assets Trusts	16.9	16.6
3.28	MoneyMart Assets	17.6	17.5
1.79	National Liquid Reserves	17.3	17.3
2.30	NRTA-AARP U.S. Government	16.1	15.7
	Money Market Trust	15.9	16.0
1.45	Oppenheimer Money Market Fund	17.8	17.8
4.60	Paine Webber Cashfund	17.0	17.0
3.05	Reserve Fund	17.4	17.5
1.05	Scudder Cash Investment Trust	17.5	17.3
4.40	Shearson Daily Dividend	17.4	17.3
2.70	T. Rowe Price Prime Reserves	17.4	17.5
Total: 93.47 billion			

*Rounded off for convenience.

Go with the Pros?

The 23 funds listed, with $93.47 billion in assets, represented two-thirds of the assets in the 129 money funds reporting to ICI.

The publicized yields do not reflect realized gains or

losses of a capital nature. But most of these funds do not try to embellish yield by trading the securities in their portfolios. Instead, they attempt to earn big money for shareholders by buying selected debt offerings that pay high interest and holding those securities until they are redeemable in full. Naturally, the published yields of money funds are neither representative of future earnings nor indicative of the fund adviser's future performance. The yields vary from business day to business day, and the yield of *any* money fund is a function of quality, maturity, and cost of operations.

I visited one of the top money pros in June 1981 and pointed out to him that Hutton's Cash Reserve Management had racked up the best yield among the billion-dollar money funds for the week ending June 17 and for the money preceding that date.

Thomas Lynch, the Hutton vice-president in charge at that time of seeing that its money fund made money, smiled and his blue eyes twinkled as he pointed out, "All money market funds are not created equal."

And indeed they are not. Nor do they perform equally well or perform with equal safety. If you adhere to the concept that bigness makes the best place to be when it comes to money management, you can go with the pros who manage the billion-dollar money funds. But I can assure you that when it comes to earning high interest for shareholders, bigness doesn't always turn out to be best.

Watching the Yield

One of the best-yielding money funds in the industry is not a billion-dollar fund. It's Value Line Cash, whose assets are only $307 million. But back on June 17, when Hutton's fund earned 18.2% for the 7-day period and 17.8% for the 30-day period ending that date, it had plenty of competition. And for the week and month ending August 4, here's how Hutton's Cash Reserve Management stacked up against Value Line Cash Fund:

	7-day	*30-day*
Cash Reserve Management	17.8%	17.6%
Value Line Cash	18.3	18.2

Where would your money grow faster?

But the amount of yield is not the only consideration in putting your money into money funds. The *quality* of the fund portfolio (the kinds and safety of the investments) should also be of great concern to you as a potential investor.

How do you know what money funds are yielding, weekly and monthly?

You can follow them weekly in large newspapers like *The New York Times* and *Chicago Tribune*, that print listings; you can subscribe to monitoring services such as *Donoghue's Money Fund Report*; or you can call the funds you are interested in and obtain the latest yield information from them. (Phone numbers for the money funds are listed in Appendix A.)

The Money Fund Prospectus

How do you find out about any specific fund? The best way is to call or send for a *prospectus*. The prospectus is a booklet designed to reveal everything you need to know about the fund, its objectives, who manages it, who distributes or promotes it, what the fund has invested in on a specific date, and so forth. When you invest in any money fund, your dollars are being constantly managed by paid professionals who are compelled to perform within the boundaries, restrictions, and guidelines printed in the prospectus of each fund. The Securities and Exchange Commission (SEC) requires that before you make any money fund investment you obtain a copy of the prospectus, which has to be less than a year old when you receive it. In addition, every time the fund makes significant changes in personnel, investment approach, or policy, a supplement (update) to the prospectus has to be mailed to all shareholders and prospects. In this manner, you should be currently informed about the objectives, basic investment policy, and conditions of risk-assumption *before* you buy any shares—*not after.*

The best advice I can give you is that, whatever you may read or hear elsewhere, you should *never send any money to any money fund until you have carefully read the fund prospectus and you are sure you understand precisely what the fund may or may not invest in your behalf.*

What to Look for in the Prospectus

When you send for any money fund prospectus, here's what you should look for:

1. *Who the distributors and directors are.* What is the background of the people who founded and operate the fund? Have they enough experience to see that the investment adviser carries out his duties as described?
2. *Who the investment advisers are.* Do they advise other funds of this nature? Ask your broker about them if you don't know yourself.
3. *What the investment restrictions are.* Each prospectus tells you in clear and comprehensible language what the advisers may invest in and what percentage of the portfolio may be invested in any specific borrower.
4. *How the assets are valued; how dividends are calculated, applied, and taxed.* There are four methods of valuing assets of money funds. But buy only those money funds that use either amortized cost or penny rounding accounting. How do you know what method is used? The prospectus tells you. The

prospectus tells you if the dividends are applied daily, compounded daily and applied once a month, etc. Do not buy any money fund shares that are not compounded daily and do not have constant $1 value. Taxes on yields received from money funds are treated as dividends. The funds of course pay no taxes because all the income after expenses is passed along daily to the shareholders.

5. *How you can buy and redeem (sell) the shares.* The prospectus reveals the minimum initial purchase permissible and the minimum subsequent purchase size. It tells you if you can purchase directly from the fund or through a brokerage account. In cases where you can buy through stockbrokers, you open a brokerage account, deposit funds, and ask your broker to buy fund shares (generally no commission). In cases where you buy direct from the fund, you must complete a proper order form and accompany this with a check in the amount desired. You can also call the fund, get an account number, and wire transfer funds from your bank to that account number at the fund's custodian bank. You can redeem (liquidate) your shares by phone, wire, or letter. And if the fund offers check-writing privileges, you can empty out any part or all of your account simply by writing a check. The check must be on the draft form sent to you by the money fund; and it must be at least $500 for most funds. Some funds automatically close your account and send you the money therein if your balance drops to $500 and remains there for some time. The prospectus will tell you if the fund follows this liquidation policy.
6. *What the expenses consist of.* All money funds have expenses. A listing of these, and of such things as the fees for investment advisory management, are

clearly indicated in the prospectus. Generally, the fees for advice and management are reduced percentagewise as the fund assets size grows. The prospectus tells all.

7. *What the investment portfolio contains.* The makeup of the investment portfolio of money market debt instruments for a specific date is illustrated in the prospectus. But if you look at the maturity dates, the chances are that these debt securities have matured and have been replaced by other securities in the money market. The prospectus does, however, provide you with an example of how much of the fund's assets are placed in each sector of the money market by the fund investment advisers. Some funds also send along a recent listing of their portfolio for examination. If you do not receive such a list when you ask for a prospectus, ask for the current investment position list. Chances are that the person answering the phone might volunteer, "We're 38% in CDs, 10% in BAs, 5% in governments, 10% in repos, and the rest in commercial paper." Each prospectus describes the various money market securities the fund is permitted to invest in. (See chapter 3 for my descriptions).
8. *Assorted financial statements.* These include income and expense statements, a balance sheet for a specific date, and voluminous explanatory notes that qualify the numbers in the statements.
9. *Methods of rating money market instruments.* This information usually appears in the prospectus as an appendix; it reveals how the fund approaches investment by using the ratings of such evaluators as Standard & Poor's or Moody's Investment Services.

After you have carefully read any money fund prospectus, you have to come away with the feeling that somebody is willing to work hard to make the most money possible for you in short-term money market debt securities—consistent with safety, according to the ratings of Standard & Poor's and Moody's. But while each fund may have similar objectives in this regard, each one functions and operates in a slightly different way, and each one invests individually, even though some funds may be managed by the same investment advisers.

In chapter 3, the kinds of investments money funds are permitted to make are explained, along with the factors that make some of them riskier than others.

Contracting a Money Fund

Money funds extend the opportunity for investors—private, institutional, and commercial—to participate in earning money from the high-interest money market. But not all funds are open to private investors. Some are available to institutions only. Nor are all the money funds "blue skyed" in every state in the union (that is, registered with the state securities commission and available to residents of that state).

For example, I have a long-standing love affair with Spokane, Washington; when I learned there was a competently managed money fund in that fair city called Composite Cash Management (a $250-million fund), I phoned and asked for a prospectus. "Where are you calling from?" a sweet voice asked.

"New York," I grumbled.

"Sorry," answered the sweet voice. "If you live in New York I cannot send you a prospectus. We're not registered in that state."

"What about Idaho?" I shot back.

"Oh. Idaho's fine," the sweet voice confirmed. "But you don't live in Idaho."

"But my son is a sophomore at Idaho University in Moscow, U.S.A.," I volunteered.

"I'll be glad to send him one if you give me his full name and address."

Incidentally, getting in touch with a money fund by phone costs nothing but your time. Mailing a newspaper coupon takes time and involves ever escalating postage costs. But be forewarned that if you call well-advertised and popular money funds on their toll-free numbers you may hear a recorded message telling you all lines are busy and "please hold on." You may hold for a long time.

So my advice is that if you have an outgoing WATS line, call the local number of the fund; if not, call collect.

Now, assuming you called the Kemper Money Market Fund, as I did in June 1981, and received the prospectus and pertinent updates, you would find an account-information form attached to the prospectus and another page of instructions indicating how you can invest and withdraw from the fund. Upon examining the order form and instructions, I found them quite clear and didn't need a lawyer to help me if I decided to invest. Incidentally, Kemper will take either individual accounts or joint accounts. In the case of a joint account opting for the check-drawing rights (Kemper calls it "redemption"), both parties have to sign; there is a space to signify whether both owners have to sign checks or either signature is acceptable. If you decide not to choose the checking privilege but will eventually sell your shares by written redemption instructions, Kemper says, "The request must be signed exactly as your account is registered and your signature must be guaranteed by a commercial bank or by a member firm of a national securities exchange."

The important thing is for you to make sure you understand what is printed on the order blank and accompanying instructions of any money fund you decide to invest in to see if you are easily able to comply with the terms of getting out as well as getting in. Understandably, funds that receive money by mail from people they do not meet face to face have to be careful that the accounts they open are, for example, for living individuals with social security numbers, or if they have applications from small businesses, IRS identification numbers. In a similar vein, the funds have to make sure they are paying out to the proper party, by mail or wire transfer. Actually, the forms required to open an account at a money fund are not any more complicated than those for opening a bank or thrift account.

Offering shareholders check-redemption privileges is an added expense to money fund operations because the fund has to print special checks (usually carbon-leaved snapout sets of checks adaptable to computer handling). To make sure they do not compete with checking accounts at banks and thrifts, money funds, with rare exceptions, do not permit redemption by check for less than $500 a check. When the check reaches the custodian bank, the fund sells enough shares to cover the draft (a $500 check would prompt liquidation of 500 shares from your money fund account).

Why Money Funds and Banks Are Both Needed

By now it should be clear that a money fund cannot operate without a bank to handle receipt and payment of money and securities—and for safekeeping of the portfolio—besides clearing the check.

And if you want to participate in the money market game by purchasing shares in a money fund, you also will need a bank or thrift somewhere along the way. While many banks and thrifts and money funds offer useful services for investors, it should be clearly understood that neither one can quite duplicate the services and functions of the other. For example, if I had all my reserve cash in a money fund and had to make a small purchase, I would have to use a $500 money fund check. To convert this piece of paper into legal tender I would have to cash the draft at a local bank or thrift. Even though I have known bank and thrift officers in my town for 34 years, I wonder how quick they would be to cash my money fund check if I didn't have on deposit at that bank or thrift at least $500 in good money (cleared funds) in my checking or savings account.

And that is just why smart investors must learn how to have the best of both worlds by utilizing money funds and banks and thrifts wisely and properly.

Money Fund Performance: Safety First, or Yield?

As I've already cautioned, you should not assume that all money funds are alike—that if Morgan Stanley or Bernstein-Macaulay is the investment adviser, you're bound to come out way ahead of the pack. Another assumption to be avoided is the widespread belief that the money funds catch up with each other and by the end of the year they have all evened out when it comes to investment performance.

Bunk.

If performance were the overriding investment objective, Value Line Cash would be much bigger in size and more popular than it is today. That fund out-performed all the money funds in 1980 and is doing it again on almost a weekly basis during 1981. But an important factor in assessing performance to suit personal requirements should also be *safety*. Thus, while all money market media invested in by money funds are classified as "low risk," some categories are safer than others, some companies have a better ability to repay promises when due than others, and some companies might not be able to repay at all and are willing to pay higher-than-going interest to renew their paper promises to repay instead of coming up with the cash when the maturity date arrives.

That is why an intelligent investor realizes that high yields should not be the *sole* reason for selecting the money fund that you hope will both make money for you and keep it safe. In the money market game the safety of your committed principal must also receive high ratings. On July 13, 1981, Value Line had 100% of its cash fund portfolio committed to commercial paper, the *riskiest* of all securities in the money market. And it was the *only* fund fully invested in such high-paying corporate paper promises to pay by a specific date.

That is why, after you read about what money funds invest in and after you examine my method of rating money funds (in Chapter 6), you'll understand my reason for rating Value Line Cash Fund tops in performance but bottoms in safety.

Money Fund Marketing Clout

Whether the primary consideration on your part when assessing a possible investment in a money fund is the yield or the degree of portfolio safety, the primary goal of money fund managements is to grow as big as possible by modern marketing methods, including advertising. The funds received a blessing from the SEC in 1981, when that government agency decided that advertising expenses, formerly the burden of the distributing company, could be charged directly to interest income. What these expenses will do to eventual yields disbursed to investors is difficult to envision at this time. But advertising has certainly worked wonders for those funds who do it regularly. And the most obvious target of those money funds that regularly advertise is the small saver, the person with $10,000 or less at banks and thrifts.

In May 1981 I called a large sampling of money funds that advertised regularly to obtain copies of their prospectuses and updated supplements. The representatives who answered my calls were all courteous, took my name and address, and mailed the requested material promptly to me. Along with the prospectus came updates, additional explanatory material—and in most cases, sales letters and notes, including an envelope labeled "No postage necessary if mailed in the United States."

Let me now caution you either to use your own envelope and stamp or to stick a postage stamp on the prepaid envelope supplied by the fund if you intend to invest. You do not begin collecting what many funds call "money market interest" until your check has been received by the fund—and in most cases, until the check clears. Obviously, the faster your check gets to the involved money fund, the faster you will begin earning high money market interest in the form of per-share dividends.

If you use the fund's envelope and first class mail return privilege, it may take almost ten days from the time you mail it until the fund even receives your application and check. Years ago, business reply mail (which is what the postage-paid envelope is supposed to be) was delivered daily by the post office. Now it's dealt with about once a week in most areas.

Advertising is one thing, and making the sale something else. Some funds use the informed investor or educational approach in their advertising, telling prospects such basic things as what a money fund is and how it earns high interest in the form of dividends. Some funds emphasize the attributes of the fund, especially the available services, in their advertising. Other funds advertise in large print the average yield of their fund for a seven-day period, along with the fine print at the bottom of the ads stating that this yield is not representative of future performance. And some funds advertise their seven-day yield and compare it with the six-month return on money market certificates issued by insured banks and thrifts.

Here is a brief breakdown of the approaches used by money funds that advertise regularly to attract new investors:

Money Fund Advertising Approaches

Fund	*Educational*	*Average yield*	*Comparisons with banks*
Fidelity		X	X
IDS	X		
Kemper	X	X	X
Dreyfus	X	X	
Lehman		X	
Delaware		X	X
Scudder		X	
Putnam	X		
Equitable	X		
T. Rowe Price		X	

Notice that seven out of the ten funds in this sampling relied on their current high yield to attract attention from potential investors, even though no money fund can guarantee the advertised yield's continuance in the future.

But I must confess that I was strongly drawn to the educational advertisement for Value Line Cash Fund that ran for many weeks in *The New York Times*. This ad invited readers to "check us out" by displaying certain attributes that every *ideal* money fund should have. And quite rightly the ad did not allude to either past or future performance. Here is the checklist displayed in the ad:

√ No Sales Charges
√ Minimum Investment Only $1,000
√ Low Management Fee (4/10 of 1%)
√ High Interest Income
√ No Cost Checks Earn Interest
√ Daily Dividends Compound Daily

√ No Cost Reinvestment Privilege
√ No Cost Cash Distribution Plans
√ Invest By Wire
√ Redeem By Wire Or Toll-free Call
√ Constant $1.00 Net Asset Value
√ No Redemption Fees
√ Managed by Arnold Bernhard & Co., Inc.

Checking the Value Line Checklist

Let's look at most of these items in the Value Line Cash Fund checklist and examine what each attribute actually means:

1. *No sales charge.* There are no charges to the investor for purchase or redemption of fund shares. But expenses are deducted from gross interest earnings. Every no-load money fund lets you in and out for free but deducts expenses from the daily income before handing it over to shareholders in the form of dividends.
2. *Minimum investment only $1,000.* Most funds of this nature have low minimums of $1,000. Some demand figures as high as $2,500 and $5,000. When Lehman Brothers Cash Fund made its debut, $10,000 represented the minimum initial investment, but this was later reduced to $5,000. Nuveen Tax Free Trust requires $25,000. (You can see the minimum initial investment required and subsequent minimum additions for each reporting ICI-member money fund in Appendix A.)
3. *High interest income.* Pirandello once noted, "If you believe it's so: it's so." The fund portfolio earns money market interest. After expenses and any net realized gains and losses, it's passed on to you as compounded dividends.
4. *Daily dividends compound daily.* All funds offer-

ing daily dividends compound them by computer. It doesn't matter if the compounding process occurs each day on the computer, or once a week, or once a month. If it's compounded daily at one fund, or less frequently but on a daily basis for the month's performance, you'll wind up with the same number of shares, if the yield is comparable.

5. *No-cost reinvestment privilege.* Value Line offers other kinds of mutual funds that carry "load charges" (front-end charges in lieu of sales commissions). If you are an investor in the Value Line Cash Fund you can at any time switch to another Value Line Fund without paying any load charge. For that matter, this free conversion privilege is available from most investment management companies that sponsor money funds and other types of mutual funds.
6. *No-cost cash distribution plans.* If you have established do-it-yourself IRA or Keogh Plan accounts and desire to draw a set amount at a determined frequency when eligible, there are no charges at Value Line; other money funds may levy a small charge (see the involved fund's prospectus).
7. *Invest by wire.* Every money fund will accept wired funds from your bank without charge. But your bank probably will levy a small charge for the service. You can find out the cost before sending the wire. If $1,000 is involved, it would earn about 44¢ a day at 17%. So chances are the wire charge would exceed the advantage of earning money market rates faster than the mail. But $100,000 would earn $44 a day—and bank wires for that amount go for a whole lot less.
8. *Redeem by wire or toll-free call.* Not every money

fund offers such services; but Value Line didn't say whether the wire redemption service was free.

9. *Constant $1.00 net asset value.* That's the only kind of money fund to invest in. Scudder Cash Investment Trust, for example, points out that this method of accounting provides a stable share price and shareholders have always been able to withdraw at least the same amount of principal they invest, even if it goes in and out of the fund the same day. Do not invest in money funds that do not offer the $1 constant net asset value.
10. *No redemption fee.* No-load funds do not have any fees on purchase or redemption.
11. *Managed by Arnold Bernhard & Co. Inc.* Here the Bernhard & Co. investment advisory services are alluded to because Bernhard is the founder of all Value Line funds and services. The prospectus of every money fund readily reveals who the fund's investment adviser is—and most experienced money fund advisers have excellent track records.

Misleading Money Fund Ads

Recently, an advertisement for a popular money fund compared a 17.25% seven-day money fund yield with the much lower 15.93% guaranteed yield of six-month, interest-bearing, insured bank money market certificates. In my opinion this ad attempted—by implication—to influence unfairly readers who might have bank money market certificates coming due, or who intended to make such a purchase, to switch to shares of a money fund, whose yield varies *every single day*. As we have seen, all money fund yields vary daily as portions of the portfolio mature and new securities are purchased, while the bank certificate locks up money for the depositor at an agreed—and sure—interest rate for six months.

It so happens that in late May 1981 some of our money market certificates at a local bank came due and my wife consulted me about whether to roll them over (renew them) for another six months or transfer the money to our money fund.

Since part of my responsibilities as research director for a global commodity firm involves interest-rate forecasting, I concluded (perhaps erroneously) that T-bill rates would drop dramatically during the second half of 1981. So we left the money invested for the next six months at an effective yield of better than 16.5% in a bank money market certificate rather than take the chance of earning better than 17% for seven days with *any* money fund.

Only a week after the roll-over, T-bill rates took a dive. During June, those rates were under 15%—and money market rates remained over 17%, because of the initial lag behind the T-bill rates in declining interest rate markets. If our money market certificates had matured during June, I certainly would have switched to the money fund to earn the 2% higher yield than the under-15% rate in June. But if the $20,000 I locked in for six months at 16.5% in the bank certificate were instead shifted to a money fund during a prolonged rate decline, I might find the money earning 12% instead of 16.5%.

On the other hand, should interest rates rise the rest of the year to the 25% or 30% levels predicted by some analysts, I can always borrow at 1% over the stated rate on my certificate and shift the cash to a money fund paying much higher dividends than the rate I'd be paying on my certificate loan. Then, when rates come down, I can liquidate my fund shares and pay off the bank loan, and so on. Incidentally, for readers who may not be familiar with interest rates, the best money fund average yield in 1980 was 12.93%, and there were occasions in 1980 when T-bill rates were higher than money fund dividend yields.

That is why smart investors should manage their

reserve money in a flexible enough manner to shift quickly with the changing trends in interest rates.

Mind you, I have nothing against any fund that advertises its weekly annualized yield for seven days and also lists the various services it offers such as checking and no-penalty withdrawals. But I do object to advertisements comparing two separate and differing situations, implying that one is better than the other. The danger is that such advertising will cause people who do not understand the true situation to draw out substantial sums of money from insured depositories and place them in uninsured, low-risk money fund shares.

Failing Depositories?

The fact is that because of aggressive advertising, extensive media publicity, and various seminars, money funds have been so well huckstered that people all over the country have begun to believe that they are bank and thrift substitutes. To add to this situation, alarming articles appeared in the press continually during the summer of 1981 about the troubles of thrift institutions and banks caused by a combination of high interest rates in the short term and demand for low interest loans for housing and business in the long term.

But there is not going to be a wholesale failing of traditional depositories such as banks and thrifts. Neither are there going to be mass bankruptcies in business sufficient to wreck our monetary system, as some doomsayers keep claiming at well-attended conferences from New Orleans to London to Australia. The Federal Reserve Board and the Federal Home Loan Bank Board have already come to the aid of their bank and thrift memberships.

Deregulatory action has raised the ceilings on bank and thrift certificates under four years from the previous 12% maximum. Now the banks and thrifts will be in a better position to compete with money funds for saving dollars. Mortgage ceilings have been lifted in many states, and innovations such as variable rate mortgages will permit thrifts to lend long-term money for mortgages at higher rates than they pay short-term depositors.

A new day is coming for the smart investor who wants to maximize reserve funds. But I sincerely hope I haven't given the impression that I personally do not like money funds or that I resent their obvious impact on previously low-paying banks or thrifts. Nothing could be further from the truth. As I confessed at the outset, my wife keeps a substantial amount of our liquid reserves in a money fund—but no more than we could afford to lose. What I have attempted to do, before moving on to explain money market debt instruments, is simply to put matters in their proper perspective so that you do not go overboard on money funds if you cannot afford to take the low risks they represent.

Money Fund Pointers

In summary, then, you should remember:

1. Money funds are mutually owned pools promoted and managed by distributors who are not philanthropists.
2. Money funds do better than bank money market certificates during periods of sustained rising short-term interest rates but fall behind bank and thrift yields if there is a long decline in short-term rates.
3. Money fund earnings vary daily. Bank or thrift money market certificate accounts offer fixed interest rates for set periods of time, and may earn investors better or worse returns than money fund dividends during a six-month or one-year period.
4. Purchases of money fund shares entail a low degree of risk; the funds have expenses, and the reported

yields in the press may be slightly overstated. Insured bank and thrift accounts are riskless.

5. Most major money funds offering checking require that the minimum size check be $500. Money fund checks are useful to pay big-ticket items since you earn dividends daily until the check appears at the money fund's bank.
6. Finally, money funds are money management tools that enable you to park liquid reserves for brief periods of time to earn high dividends with low risk while waiting to put the reserves to use elsewhere.

So that you may become familiar with the various kinds of short-term investments money funds participate in almost daily, let's now look at major money market debt instruments.

3

What You Should Know About the Money Market

On June 3, 1981, the United States needed cash so urgently that it issued and sold millions upon millions of dollars' worth of "cash management bills"—with a maturity of 15 days. The annual rate of interest on these bills was a record 18.5%. Never before had our government paid so much for an obligation considered by experts in finance as *completely riskless*.

Where did our profligate government go to raise the cash required to meet the so-called emergency.

The money market.

Just what is the money market? It's where the federal government, states, municipalities, and big business go to change paper promises to pay at a future date into ready cash. For this conversion from promises to money, the borrowers, of course, pay interest on the debt, or sell the face value of the debt at a discount. The rate of interest paid to the lender depends on many factors, including the lender's assessment of the borrower's ability to pay the debt when due.

Basically, the money market is a market that spreads around the world from New York City, where government and corporate borrowers can apply for short-term (up to two years), intermediate-term (two to ten years), and long-term funds (ten years and up). To service government, banking and corporate short-term money needs (the area of financing that primarily concerns us here), a network of banks, securities dealers, financial firms like Citibank and Commercial Credit, and nonfinancial firms like Westinghouse Electric maintain departments, or "money centers," specializing in buying and selling money market debt instruments.

Money Market Debt Categories

Most money market debt instruments fall into one of four broad categories: (1) government, (2) municipal, (3) bank, and (4) corporate. Because municipal debt is a highly specialized area that normally involves much longer time periods to maturity than the short-term debts being considered here, I am not going into detail in this book about its benefits and dangers. But the other three categories of debt are of direct concern to investors eying the money market hoping to earn high interest rates either by direct investment in the debt instruments available or indirectly through money funds.

The government debt for short-term purposes is in turn divided into the following major categories:

1. *T-bills* (Treasury bills) for three months, six months and one year
2. *Government bonds* and *notes* maturing within one year
3. Obligations of federal agencies such as the FHA (Federal Housing Administration) and the SBA (Small Business Administration)
4. *Repurchase agreements* (repos or RPs) and *reverse repurchase agreements* (reverses)

Bank debt consists mainly of *certificates of deposit* and *banker's acceptances.*

Corporate short-term debt consists of *commercial paper* and *corporate notes.*

Let's now look more closely at the composite parts of these major money market categories.

Treasury Bills (T-Bills)

The most popular participant in the government sector of the money market game is the T-bill. The Treasury, through the Federal Reserve System, auctions billions of dollars worth of T-bills every Monday for three- and six-month maturities. Every 28 days, it also auctions T-bills that mature in a year.

The T-bill itself is bought and retired upon maturity by book entry. This means there is no physical certificate issued by the government; instead, the account of the primary bank or securities dealer who takes down the T-bills at the auction is debited by the Federal Reserve Bank of New York (N.Y. Fed) upon purchase and credited upon maturity. Basically, the T-bill is a discounted obligation of the government that is repaid at face value upon maturity. Minimum purchase is $10,000 face value.

If you purchased $10,000 worth of three-month T-bills through your bank, broker, or direct from the Federal Reserve at an average discount at the auction of 15.46%, your actual cost would have been $9,609.20—and at the end of the three-month period, you'd cash the bills in for precisely $10,000. In essence, you are not using $10,000 to earn the reward inherent in the T-bill purchase; instead, you are investing only $9,609.20, which will earn you interest of $390.80 in three months. Theoretically, if interest rates remained level for the three-month period, your T-bill purchase would be worth exactly $4.34 more per day, as each day passed, until by the ninetieth day the T-bill would be worth $10,000. But because rates change weekly, if you sold your T-bills before maturity you'd find the $4.34/day increment higher or lower at time of sale.

In addition to the primary market, where newly issued T-bills are auctioned every week, there exists a very active secondary market trading old bills that have not yet matured. This T-bill market is conducted among the N.Y. Fed recognized banks and dealers, and their correspondent banks and dealers all over the world on behalf of themselves or their customers.

The Federal Reserve issues weekly lists of outstanding T-bills available to investors at banks, brokers, and dealers, and quotations appear in major financial media. But unlike the listings of government notes and coupon bonds, numbers in the newspapers pertaining to T-bills, traded at a discount from par, and for government bonds and notes traded at a percentage of par, are quite different. Here is a typical T-bill listing in the secondary market from *The New York Times* of August 14, 1981:

Date (1981)	*Bid*	*Ask*	*Change*	*Yield*
Sept. 17	15.48	15.22	−0.15	15.64

The first entry on the left identifies the T-bill maturity date. The second column, "Bid," reflects the discount yield a dealer would accept if you wanted to sell such a bill to him. The third column, "Ask," reflects the discount you would receive if you bought the bill from the dealer. The fourth column identifies the net change in the yield from the previous listing; the final column reflects the equivalent yield if the obligation were an interest-bearing bond or note and would be held at that return for one year.

In order to convert what you see in the newspapers into actual cost, you need formulas that will permit you to readily estimate the proper value of an outstanding T-bill for any maturity and determine its coupon yield equivalent. I have provided such calculation methods in the next chapter, which explains money market math.

Because of the volatility of interest rates, the normal daily increase in value of maturing T-bills may be slowed or accelerated. So if you buy six-month bills and decide to sell them after a very brief holding period, you might wind up with a loss. Conversely, in times when interest rates suddenly shoot up, you can buy outstanding bills at a better discount than they were issued at and resell them in the secondary market for profits when rates drop. The accrual of money from the purchase price at a discount to the full face value at maturity is considered income, not gain. And because T-bills—and only T-bills—are considered "nonfinancial assets" by the IRS, losses from sale of actual bills are considered deductions from income, not capital losses for investors.

Actually, you can never lose any money on *any* T-bills if you hold them to maturity, but you can increase your yield if you put the discount from, say, a $10,000 bill into a money fund at time of purchase to earn more money on the discount via daily compounded money fund dividends while the bills are aging to maturity.

In the money market, T-bills are considered the safest and most liquid obligation of the federal government, since they are direct obligations. The government sells them to make sure the Treasury is supplied with short-term cash for various needs, including massive refundings of maturing T-bills. Two things are certain: there will always be weekly T-bill auctions (unless and until some better means of supplying the government with a steady flow of money on a weekly basis comes along); and any saver or investor holding bills will receive face value on maturity date. Investors living in states that levy an annual income tax have an advantage in buying T-bills because T-bill yields are exempt from all state (but not federal) taxation.

Government Bonds and Notes

While T-bills account for the largest amount of debt issued by the government weekly in the money market, notes and bonds are important debt instruments as well. These obligations are staggered so that they: come due in one year or less; come due after one year but within five years; come due after five years but within ten years; or come due after ten years.

After these various notes and bonds are newly issued in the primary market through the network of banks, dealers, and brokers, they are available for trading and resale in the network of dealers in the secondary market. Thus investors can buy short-, medium-, and long-term government notes and bonds and resell them the same day or several days later at profits or losses, depending upon market conditions.

The prices of these government securities swing on the level of going interest rates. A list of the prices of marketable issues is made available each afternoon by the N.Y. Fed in its "Composite Closing Quotations for U.S. Securities Report," and versions of this report appear in financial sections of leading newspapers. The following table is extracted from the listing for August 11, 1981:

Composite Closing Quotations for U.S. Government Securities As of August 11, 1981
U.S. Treasury Notes and Bonds

Issue		*Bid*	*Ask*	*Change*	*Yield*
9 ⅝	8/31/81–N	99.17	21	0	16.01
6 ¾	9/30/81–N	98.16	20	0	17.05
10 ⅛	9/30/81–N	99.1	5	0	16.09
12 ⅝	10/31/81–N	98.28	0	0	16.84
7	11/15/81–N	97.14	18	+ 2	16.66
7 ¾	11/15/81–N	97.19	23	+ 1	16.74

(continued)

Issue			Bid	Ask	Change	Yield
12 ⅛	11/30/81–N		98.17	21	+ 1	16.45
7 ¼	12/31/81–N		96.20	24	+ 1	16.18
11 ⅜	12/31/81–N		98.2	6	+ 2	16.22
11 ½	1/31/82–N		97.22	26	0	16.50
6 ⅛	2/15/82–N		95.3	7	+ 3	16.36
6 ⅜	2/15/82		95.3	11	+ 3	16.34
13 ⅞	2/28/82–N		98.22	26	+ 2	16.22
7 ⅞	3/31/82–N		94.30	2	+ 2	16.38
15	3/31/82–N		99.4	8	+ 2	16.29
11 ⅜	4/30/82–N		96.20	24	+ 3	16.34
7	5/15/82–N		93.18	26	+ 6	15.96
8	5/15/82–N		94.7	15	+ 5	16.02
9 ¼	5/15/82–N		94.28	0	+ 3	16.52
9 ⅜	5/31/82–N		94.23	27	+ 3	16.50
8 ¼	6/30/82–N		93.19	23	+ 3	16.16
8 ⅝	6/30/82–N		93.26	30	+ 4	16.27
8 ⅞	7/31/82–N		93.20	24	+ 4	16.12
8 ⅛	8/15/82–N		93.2	10	+ 8	15.56
9	8/15/82–N		93.22	30	+ 8	15.75
6 ⅜	8/15/84		79.12	12	+ 16	14.68
7 ¼	8/15/84–N		82.20	28	+ 8	14.48
13 ¼	8/15/84–N		95.4	8	+ 12	15.27
12 ⅛	9/30/84–N		92.4	12	+ 15	15.27
16	11/15/84–N	WI	101.15	19	+ 15	15.35
14	12/31/84–N		96.24	0	+ 20	15.17
8	2/15/85–N		82.1	17	+ 8	14.54
13 ⅜	3/31/85–N		94.27	31	+ 14	15.23
3 ¼	5/15/85		81.14	14	- 30	8.86
4 ¼	5/15/75–85		81.2	2	- 16	10.10
10 ⅜	5/15/85–N		87.20	28	+ 3	14.68
14 ⅜	5/15/85–N		98.6	14	+ 8	14.94
14	6/30/85–N		96.30	2	+ 22	15.03
8 ¼	8/15/85–N		80.31	7	+ 11	14.61
9 ⅝	8/15/85–N		85.0	8	+ 12	14.62
11 ¾	11/15/85–N		90.0	8	+ 8	14.92
13 ½	2/15/86–N		95.5	13	+ 16	14.94
7 ⅞	5/15/86–N		78.5	13	+ 15	14.28
13 ¾	5/15/86–N		95.22	30	+ 11	14.97
8	8/15/86–N		77.23	31	+ 5	14.31
6 ⅛	11/15/86		72.2	2	+ 7	13.43
13 ⅞	11/15/86–N		96.20	24	+ 22	14.79
9	2/15/87–N		80.1	9	+ 24	14.29
12	5/15/87–N		90.17	25	+ 15	14.41

SOURCE: Federal Reserve Bank of New York, Market Reports Division.

There are six groups of numbers under the five headings of this table for each note and bond, and to show you how to read them, I have extracted the issue underlined in the table as follows:

Issue		*Bid*	*Ask*	*Change*	*Yield*
7¼	12/31/81–N	96.20	24	+1	16.18

The two numbers under the heading "Issue" identify the bond or note. In this example, the interest rate is 7¼% annually on $1,000 (par value of 100) until the maturity date of December 31, 1981. And the debt instrument here is a *note*, as identified by the letter *N* following the maturity date.

The number under the title "Bid" is the price for which a buyer is willing to purchase this note from anyone owning it; and the "Ask" is the current offer if you want to buy it from a broker or dealer. Notes and bonds are quoted in thirty-seconds of a point, with a point equaling $10; therefore, one-thirty-second equals 31.25¢. To analyze the bid and asked price of the note above, the bid of 96.20 represents 96 times $10, or $960, plus the 20 points times $0.3125, which amounts to $6.25. Thus the dealer would bid $966.25 for the note if he wanted to buy it, and offer the note at the asked price of 96.24, which amounts to 96 × $10 = $960, plus the 24 points times 31.25¢ = $7.50, or a price of $967.50. The dealer therefore could make a "spread" of $1.25 per $1,000 worth of notes, or one-eighth. This is seemingly insignificant, but if $100 million is involved, the spread is $125,000.

About $10 billion in T-bills, government bonds and notes are traded every business day in the money market, and the bulk of these secondary market transactions occurs among money market banks, dealers, and brokers who buy and sell these securities after original issuance for their accounts or for customer accounts. Because the bonds and notes are, like T-bills, a direct obligation of the government, their safety of principal and payment of coupon interest is highly ranked.

Agency Paper

In the parlance of the money market, all debt instruments are referred to professionally as "paper." Thus obligations of government agencies are referred to as "agency paper" and generate interest payments to purchasers.

This category, which is to all intents and purposes backed by the full faith and credit of the government, consists of paper that becomes a debt of the government if the agency defaults in payment of interest and principal, and paper that becomes an obligation of the government only after agency assets are exhausted. Although this may seem like a hairline of difference, and payment would probably be made in full for any agency paper in default, the question of payment time enters the picture.

Agency paper backed by the full faith and credit of the government would be redeemed quickly. Payment on paper backed specifically only by the agency could be stalled until the agency's assets were liquidated.

Since default by any government agency is possible but rather improbable, investors have come to believe that all agency obligations are safe.

Government agency obligations issued and traded in the short-term money market are assessed on the quality (ability to repay) of the issuer of the paper. This hinges on past performance of the involved borrower. Understandably, interest rates on agency issues are higher than yields on T-bills or interest on government bonds and notes, which are direct—not second- or third-hand—debts of our interest-burdened government.

Repos and Reverses

To achieve its monetary policy objectives, the Federal Reserve buys and sells outstanding government and agency obligations in the open market. Among its tools is the repurchase agreement (repo or RP). To effect a repo, the N.Y. Fed, which conducts open market operations for the Federal Reserve System, buys a government security from a dealer who agrees to repurchase the obligation in a very short period of time (usually 1 to 7 days, but at times as long as 15 days). When the dealer repurchases the security from the N.Y. Fed he pays the original price, plus an agreed yield to the Reserve Bank. This action by the Fed supplies funds to the market, or increases financial reserves.

When the N.Y. Fed sells government securities to the dealers to withdraw cash from the outstanding reserves with the agreement to sell the securities back to the dealers at the sale price plus an agreed yield to the dealers, this reverse process of a repo is called a reverse repurchase agreement (or reverse repo, or simply a reverse). When these transactions are effected, the open market desk at the N.Y. Fed generally buys back the securities involved from the dealers at an agreed yield.

From the standpoint of safety, repos rank closely with government debt and are found in growing numbers in portfolios of money funds and other large investors.

Banker's Acceptances

Banker's acceptances are negotiable instruments that are issued to finance the export, import, shipment, or storage of goods. This form of money market activity involves time drafts, which are orders to pay a specific amount of money on a certain date at maturity. The bank that these drafts are drawn on "accepts" responsibility for payment at maturity on behalf of its customer, who is, of course, obligated to pay the bank for the amount financed on or before the maturity date. This banker's acceptance, known as BA, is (like a T-bill) a discount instrument; it runs from 30 to 180 days (usually 90 days), is in bearer form, and is backed by both the bank and the borrowers involved. The dealer market in BAs involves 10 to 15 nationwide firms that also engage in buying and selling government securities. Most of the dealers are located in New York City.

Since BAs are issued as drafts by large banks who are responsible for prompt payment at maturity, and since they are also backed by the borrowers—with collateralized merchandise—this form of paper ranks high with regard to safety and generally carries a lower interest yield than the prime rate. BAs are, therefore, quite safe and highly liquid money market investments.

Certificates of Deposit

CDs, as these short-term debt instruments are called, are issued by commercial banks and thrifts for a variety of purposes, including making the borrowed funds yield higher rates to the borrowing banks than those paid to the initial lenders. While some CDs can be sold to investors in amounts as small as $25,000, most of the paper is considerably larger. These CDs are simply promissory notes for amounts of $100,000 and higher and are generally of brief duration (30 to 120 days). That is why it is not at all unusual for a bank to pay the T-bill rate on sums from $10,000 up to $99,999 and pay the substantially higher federal funds rate for 30 days on a CD. Fed funds represent the monies loaned from one bank to another overnight, or for a very short duration through the Federal Reserve.

For example in June at one savings bank I found a money market certificate based on the T-bill rate of

14.85% for deposits of at least $10,000; but the same institution was prepared to pay 18.3% for "Jumbo CDs" ($100,000 and up) with a one-month maturity.

CDs are divided into several categories:

1. *Domestic CDs,* which are obligations of banks located inside the United States
2. *Eurodollar CDs,* which are obligations of foreign-based branches of American banks such as Bankers Trust, Chase, Chemical, and Citibank
3. *Foreign CDs* (also called Yankees), which are CDs sold in American markets by American-based branches of global foreign banks, such as Barclay's

CDs of the strongest and soundest American banks pay the least interest, while the shakiest ones pay the most. Eurodollar CDs sold in foreign markets are riskier than domestic CDs and therefore carry higher interest rates.

Large investors, such as institutional investors or money funds, are quite active in domestic CDs in a highly selective manner. But there are times when these investors want to become more aggressive and less conservative in their approach to earning money market interest, and they accordingly alter their standards slightly. For example, on May 1, 1981, Fidelity Cash Reserves issued a supplement to its prospectus of March 30, 1981, telling shareholders that the trustees of the trust had determined to include in the fund's CD purchases CDs of banks and thrifts with capital, surplus and undivided profits of $100 million and less provided such instruments are insured by the FDIC and the FSLIC. It went on to point out that the rate of interest paid "on such certificates of deposits issued by such institutions is negotiable."

Such negotiations probably depend on the old maxim that "the rate is set by the party most anxious to do the business." Before May 1, 1981, Fidelity Cash could deal only in CDs of major banks, including "U.S. dollar-denominated obligations of foreign branches of U.S. banks and U.S. branches of foreign banks." Obviously, the new policy set forth in the supplement represented a broadening of the fund adviser's ability to continue to receive high interest in competition with other large money funds already acquiring CDs of banks with less than $100 million capital, surplus, and undivided profits.

Emphasizing the risks involved in purchase of Eurodollar CDs, Equitable Money Market Account, a money fund connected with the Equitable Life Assurance Society, warned its investors that the risks include "future political and economic developments, the possible imposition of United Kingdom withholding taxes on income payable on the securities [most Eurodollars CDs trade in London], the possible seizure of nationalization of foreign deposits, the possible establishment of exchange controls or the adoption of other foreign government restrictions which might adversely affect the payment of principal and interest on the Eurodollar CDs."

At least the shareholders in Equitable, and prospective buyers of its shares, were more fully informed by Equitable about Eurodollar CD risks than were shareholders of Fidelity.

Private investors can participate in the domestic and the European CD market by transactions through their brokers or banks. And these agents can supply lists of what securities of this nature are available in the secondary, or resale, market.

Commercial Paper and Corporate Notes

Commercial paper—that is, promises to repay backed by the full faith and credit of the borrowing corporation—generally run from one month (30 days) to one year. Like T-bills, commercial paper is usually sold at a discount rather than on a coupon basis, as are corporate notes, bonds and other obligations.

Commercial paper, therefore, represents a promise to pay principal backed by the good name and financial soundness of the borrowing corporation. Actually, this form of financing involves an unsecured promissory note, sold by the borrowing corporation as an alternative to borrowing money from a bank or other lending institution.

Today more than eight hundred companies in the United States regularly issue commercial paper. These issuers are

1. *Financial companies*, which are firms engaged in commercial, savings, and mortgage banking; sales, personal, and mortgage financing; factoring, finance leasing, and other business lending; insurance underwriting and other investment activities
2. *Nonfinancial companies*, which are manufacturers, industrial concerns, utility companies, and service industries

The financial companies account for 70% of all commercial paper issued and outstanding, nonfinancial companies for the remaining 30%.

Interest on commercial paper generally runs lower than bank prime lending rates, providing companies with the attractive advantage of being able to obtain lower-cost money from the money market than they can from traditional banking sources.

On July 10, 1981, the prime rate (the rate banks extend to their best borrowers) stood at 20½%. General Motors Acceptance Corporation at that time placed some paper at 17¼% for 30 to 59 days. On that same date high-grade unsecured paper placed by other major corporations threw off yields of 18.4% for 30 days and 18.1% for 60 days, and Eurodollar CDs were going at 20¼%.

Daily interest rates, on a discount basis, for paper with maturities of 30 days to 120 days are published by the N.Y. Fed and printed in the usual newspapers.

Three organizations currently rate the bulk of outstanding commercial paper:

1. Standard & Poor's assigns ratings of A-1, A-2, or A-3.
2. Moody's Investment Services assigns ratings of P-1, P-2, or P-3 (P stands for Prime).
3. Fitch uses F-1, F-2, or F-3 (F is for Fitch).

In all cases, the ratings assign the highest quality paper a 1 and the lowest quality a 3. The ratings are reviewed often and involve assessment of the corporation's ability to repay and other factors. Not all commercial paper is rated by these three firms. If the quality doesn't stack up to the standards for the ratings, the services will not rate the issues, which are then considered "unrated".

To understand what goes into these ratings, here's how Moody's qualifies a P-1 rating. P-1 is the highest Moody rating and is arrived at if the paper of the issuer meets the standards for this rating in the following areas:

1. Management evaluation of the issuer
2. Evaluation of the issuer's industry and appraisal of the speculative risks inherent in areas of that industry
3. Evaluation of issuer's products in relation to both competition and customer acceptance
4. Liquidity of the issuing corporation
5. Amount and quality of corporation debt
6. Earnings trend over the past ten years
7. Financial strength and any relationship of a corporate parent of the issuer
8. Performance of management in areas of public interest

Knowing the ratings of the commercial paper positioned in an institutional or private portfolio should be part of the investor's selection process; the higher the quality, the lower the interest—*and the less the risk of possible default.*

The same companies that issue commercial paper also issue from time to time corporate notes or obligations. These are short-term affairs of a promissory nature that return interest plus principal to the lender. Because the distinction between the issuance of corporate notes and of commercial paper is merely interest-bearing instruments (corporate notes) compared with discounted instruments (commercial paper), they bear the same quality and safety, or lack of safety, connotations and are considered part of the commercial paper world.

You can arrive at costs and yields for discounted commercial paper with the same formulas you will find in the next chapter for use in T-bill calculations.

Ingredients of a Money Market Portfolio

Now that you have been introduced briefly to the debt instruments that make up the modern money market, the obvious question is, How you can go about constructing a viable portfolio seeking high interest coupled with low risk safety?

In the first place it takes an awful lot of money. In the money market, the best deals in governments may take over a million dollars; in the banker's acceptance area, minimums are generally $500,000. The same goes for repos. Top-quality commercial paper could be purchased with $100,000 or more, but here again it takes millions of dollars to get the best deals with the greatest degree of safety.

If you are fortunate enough to have sufficient funds to

do direct purchasing in the money market yourself, I have devised a rating scale for your use in assessing the safety of any money market portfolio. T-bills, with the lowest number, have the lowest risk of default and nonpayment, while commercial paper and corporate notes, rated 9, have the highest risk.

1. T-bills
2. Other government bonds and notes
3. Government agency obligations
4. Repos
5. Banker's acceptances
6. Bank certificates of deposit (domestic CDs)
7. Domestic Eurodollar CDs and debt
8. Foreign Eurodollar CDs and debt (including Yankee bonds)
9. Commercial paper and corporate notes

Now ask yourself, "If I were a rich man or woman and wanted to risk $100 million in the money market, what would be my primary consideration?"

If the answer is safety, and no other consideration, you would assemble $100 million worth of T-bills and government notes and bonds—*the most conservative approach.*

If the answer involves a sensible degree of safety with more risk than absolute safety, or what might be termed a "happy medium," then you could divide the money equally into governments, Repos, BAs, and major bank CDs.

If your investment objective is more aggressive than a happy medium between safety and risk, you might position 50% CDs, 25% Eurodollar CDs (domestic and foreign), and 25% commercial paper and corporate notes.

Now, if safety is not your prime consideration and yield maximization is, your portfolio could be composed entirely of items 7, 8, and 9 on my list, or you can do as some money funds do and concentrate most of your portfolio in commercial paper and corporate bonds and notes.

Not all of us have $100 million to get the best deals available in the $800 billion+ money market, but some of us do have sums of $1,000, $5,000 or $25,000, that we can pool with other people into money fund investments that will perform almost as well as those million-dollar deals.

But before examining what the money funds do with the $140 billion invested in their money market portfolios, let's take a look at some easy money market math.

4

Money Market Math Made Easy

I realized long ago that it pays to learn how to add correctly and make simple multiplication calculations. And because I am essentially lazy, I have devised various short cuts for myself involving numerical estimates. Here's one of the simple ways I put this technique to work.

An aggressive supermarket in my area recently advertised certain discount merchandise that included, among other "specials," ice cream (half-gallon) normally selling for $1.69 on sale at 99¢ and orange juice (also a half-gallon), normally $1.39, for 99¢. To get the special discount prices, you had to redeem coupons appearing in the ad.

Knowing how essential it is in times of high interest rates to keep every available dollar working, I decided to take advantage of the specials and save some shopping money. So I drove over to the store, bought the specials (limit one to a customer) and also some very nice-looking fresh peaches at a very reasonable 29¢ a pound. At the checkout, where I'm usually very careful to watch each and every item rung up by the cashier, my attention happened to be drawn to a woman wearing a provocative T-shirt when I heard the cashier say, "That's $3.90."

The numbers shocked me out of my mental numbness and I countered with, "It can't be. How much are the peaches?"

"Eighty-two cents," replied the cashier.

"Well then," I volunteered, "the bill has to be less than $3. In fact, it's $2.80."

Upon checking the register tape, the cashier realized she had not deducted the $1.10 worth of coupons.

How did I know the bill was wrong? Because I have developed a short-cut method of math that I use for food shopping that told me it had to be wrong.

In this case there were three items: two of them were priced at 99¢ each and the price of the third item was unknown. I calculated mentally that each 99¢ item was $1; and when the peaches were weighed, I'd simply deduct 2¢ from their cost and have the exact cost of my shopping trip. That is how I came up with the $2.80 figure after I knew the 82¢ cost of the peaches.

Rounding figures to the nearest dollar is just one of the many devices one can develop in making math easy. Learning how to use a pocket calculator or a desk-top calculator, with or without a tape, is another.

In the money market world, calculators and computers abound, along with people who know how to use them accurately and effectively.

Simple Interest Calculations

Money market people face a myriad of problems in their approach to high interest earnings for themselves, for customers, or both.

The basics of solving money market problems—outside of when to buy or sell for profits or losses—involve *interest and yield*. The problems are composed of:

1. The amount borrowed or loaned
2. The return to the lender
3. The length of time until payment
4. The terms of interest on the principal and/or the size of the discount from the face value

To the manager of a money market portfolio, the investment of *X* dollars into selected securities will grow into more dollars today; and these dollars have to grow into more dollars tomorrow. The attainment of investment objectives of low risk coupled with high income depends upon the performance of the person attempting to solve money market problems.

The first important item is the knowledge that *all interest* earned by owners of money market debt instruments is *simple interest*. If you lend a local bank $100,000 for a 30-day CD at 18% annually, you'll receive your $100,000 at maturity (say 30 days) plus *one month's interest* at the annual rate of 18%. This interest amounts to $1,500. You've invested it for one month and now the note comes due and you have earned at an annual rate of 18%, but your money has been at work earning you money only for one month!

If one made the rather bizarre assumption that you did nothing at all with the funds for the next eleven months, the annual rate you would have earned would not be 18%; it would be 1.5%.

Now how did I know quickly—and without involved mathematical calculations—that $100,000 at 18% annual interest working for one month would be $1,500?

There are at least five ways to find the correct answer to this problem.

1. *The sharp-pencil method.* First figure the annual interest on the $100,000 principal; then divide the result by the number of months in the year to find the interest cost to the borrower for one month's use of the money at 18% annual rate.

$$\$100{,}000 \times .18 \text{ (percents are expressed in decimals)} \times \text{one year } (1) = \frac{\$18{,}000}{12 \text{ months}} = \$1{,}500 \text{ for one month.}$$

2. *The 60-day-6% method.* In this method, the simple interest on *any amount* loaned at a 6% simple interest annual rate for 60 days (two months in a 360-day year) is the principal amount with a decimal moved two places to the left. Since the loan is $100,000, the 60-day-6% interest would be $1,000. But 18% is three times the 6% rate, so at the 18% rate you'd multiply the $1,000 by three, arriving at $3,000 interest for two months. Since the money is to be used only for one month (half that time), you divide this in half and arrive at $1,500 for one month.
3. *The short-cut method.* The way I would do it is to move the decimal three places to the left on the principal of $100,000, arriving at 6% interest for 6 days (10% of the amount for 60 days). With five 6-day periods in a month and a rate of 18%, or three times the 6% rate, I'd multiply the $100, 6-day-at-6% figure by 15 and reach $1,500. I got the factor of 15 by multiplying the number of time periods of 6 days each in a 30-day month (5) by the number of times the rate 18% is higher than the 6% (3).
4. *The academic method.* This method, of course, involves a formula. The standard formula is S = A (1 + in), explained as follows:

   S = the resulting dollar amount owed
   A = the amount of the loan in dollars
   i = the annual simple interest rate
   n = the number of years involved

   To find S in the foregoing problem the formula would be:

   $$S = 100{,}000\ (1 + .18 \times 1/12) = \$101{,}500$$

   Thus, the interest earned for one month (one-twelfth of a year) is $1,500 after subtracting the $100,000 principal.

5. *The quick-calculator method.* This method, a favorite of company treasurers and of mine, involves examination of daily interest on any interest problem. Since we are dealing in this problem with a 360-day year, the first thing would be to determine the annual interest, in this case $100,000 times .18, or $18,000. Having found this the treasurer would divide the $18,000 annual interest by 360 and multiply the result by 30 days as follows:

$$\frac{\$18{,}000}{360} \times 30 = \$1{,}500$$

What has actually been done is that the *daily* interest at the annualized rate has been determined simply by dividing the 360 days into the annual interest and arriving at $50 a day. Then the number of days are multiplied by the daily interest to arrive at the answer. Now that you know the daily interest earning on the $100,000 principal at 18% is $50, how much would a lender earn on that principal and on that interest rate for a week (seven days)? The answer is $350, or seven days times the daily interest of $50. The importance of this method becomes evident when you want to know how much you could earn for one week on $14,000 throwing off an annual yield of 17.29%. Try it on your calculator.

All the preceding methods of calculating simple interest are workable when it comes to calculating return on investment in such money market instruments as certificates of deposit, government notes and bonds, and corporate notes and bonds. The quick-calculator method (#5) is the most widely used. Remember: multiply the principal (the amount you intend to pay for a money market debt instrument of any of these categories) by the interest rate (interest followed by a percent sign is expressed decimally in hundredths). Then divide by 360 *if annual interest* is concerned, or 365 *if annualized interest* is desired to get the daily interest. Then multiply by the number of days to maturity or disposal to find the amount of interest you can expect for your risk in that particular instrument.

Discount Yield Calculations

The earnings from such discounted debt instruments as T-bills, banker's acceptances, and most commercial paper cannot be calculated in the same way that simple interest is. Instead, formulas are used to determine the return on investment in these discounted securities. The keys to finding your earnings from a discounted instrument involve: (a) determining the discount; (b) finding the actual cost of the instrument; and (c) relating the reward to the equivalent interest that would have been earned in a coupon bond.

Here then are the rudiments of the T-bill math.

Determining the Discount

The popular T-bills auctioned every week include three-month and six-month bills. The three-month bills may be 90, 91, or 92 days; the six-month bills are 26 weeks, or 182 days. The minimum bill sold at auction is $10,000, and since about $8 billion worth of bills are auctioned weekly, the government can accommodate larger investors. But I am using $10,000 as the figure in the following examples.

The formula for determining the discount on a three-month bill is:

$$\frac{\text{Days to maturity} \times \text{Discount rate yield} \times \$10{,}000}{360} = \text{Discount}$$

Thus, to find the discount on a T-bill for 90 days with a Fed discount rate of 15%, the formula becomes:

$$\frac{90 \times .15 \times \$10{,}000}{360} = \$375$$

And if you want to determine the discount on a T-bill at the same 15% figure, but for a 91-day bill, you work it out as follows:

$$\frac{91 \times .15 \times \$10{,}000}{360} = \$379.17$$

Thus we've found that the cost to a buyer of the 90-day bill would be $10,000, less the $375 discount, or $9,-625.00. And the cost to the buyer of a 91-day bill at the 15% discount rate would be $9,620.83, or $4.17 less.

The same could be done for a 92-day bill, but there are, of course, short cuts. Having found the discount for the 90-day bill at 15% to be precisely $375, I'd divide that figure by the number of days in the bill, or 90, to ascertain the daily increment of increase of $4.1666666, or (rounded off) $4.17. Since the T-bill obviously becomes more valuable for each day nearer to maturity by the the amount of the daily increment, to get the 91-day bill cost I'd substract the $4.17 from the 90-day cost.

An even simpler way to find the discount and the cost of a 91-day bill at 15% is to look it up in a table such as the one supplied by the International Monetary Market (IMM) of the Chicago Mercantile Exchange (see following table). Since the IMM trades T-bill futures in million-dollar contract lots, all you have to do is move the decimal two places to the left in the figures found in the table to come up with the discount and the cost basis of a $10,000 T-bill.

91-Day U.S. Treasury Bills 14.91% to 15.41% Discount Rates

Discount rate	*Coupon equivalent*	*Discount on $1,000,000*	*Price*
15.41	16.257	38,953.06	961,046.94
15.40	16.246	38,927.78	961,072.22
15.39	16.235	38,902.50	961,097.50
15.38	16.224	38,877.22	961,122.78
15.37	16.213	38,851.94	961,148.06
15.36	16.202	38.826.67	961,173.33
15.35	16.191	38,801.39	961,198.61
15.34	16.180	38,776.11	961,223.89
15.33	16.169	38,750.83	961,249.17
15.32	16.159	38,725.56	961,274.44
15.31	16.148	38,700.28	961,299.72
15.30	16.137	38,675.00	961,325.00
15.29	16.126	38,649.72	961,350.28
15.28	16.115	38,624.44	961,375.56
15.27	16.104	38,599.17	961,400.83
15.26	16.093	38,573.89	961,426.11
15.25	16.082	38,548.61	961,451.39
15.24	16.071	38,523.33	961,476.67
15.23	16.060	38,498.06	961,501.94
15.22	16.049	38,472.78	961,527.22
15.21	16.038	38,447.50	961,552.50
15.20	16.027	38,422.22	961,577.78
15.19	16.016	38,396.94	961,603.06
15.18	16.005	38,371.67	961,628.33
15.17	15.994	38,346.39	961,653.61
15.16	15.983	38,321.11	961,678.89
15.15	15.972	38,295.83	961,704.17
15.14	15.961	38,270.56	961,729.44
15.13	15.950	38,245.28	961,754.72
15.12	15.939	38,220.00	961,780.00
15.11	15.928	38,194.72	961,805.28
15.10	15.917	38,169.44	961,830.56
15.09	15.906	38,144.17	961,855.83
15.08	15.895	38,118.89	961,881.11
15.07	15.884	38,093.61	961,906.39
15.06	15.873	38,068.33	961,931.67

(continued)

Discount rate	*Coupon equivalent*	*Discount on $1,000,000*	*Price*
15.05	15.862	38,043.06	961,956.94
15.04	15.852	38,017.78	961,982.22
15.03	15.841	37,992.50	962,007.50
15.02	15.830	37,967.22	962,032.78
15.01	15.819	37,941.94	962,058.06
15.00	15.808	37,916.67	962,083.33
14.99	15.797	37,891.39	962,108.61
14.98	15.786	37,866.11	962,133.89
14.97	15.775	37,840.83	962,159.17
14.96	15.764	37,815.56	962,184.44
14.95	15.753	37,790.28	962,209.72
14.94	15.742	37,765.00	962,235.00
14.93	15.731	37,739.72	962,260.28
14.92	15.720	37,714.44	962,285.56
14.91	15.709	37,689.17	962,310.83

NOTE: This table is reproduced from a booklet entitled 91-Day U.S. Treasury Bills—6% to 20% Discount Rates, published by the International Monetary Market (IMM) division of the Chicago Mercantile Exchange. It is available free from the IMM at 444 West Jackson Blvd. Chicago, Ill. 60606.

In chapter 3, I mentioned a T-bill offering listed in *The New York Times* and said you'd need to use a formula to calculate how much that bill would actually cost. The maturing bill was at 15.22 "Ask," the price you'd probably have to pay, plus a small commission. Disregarding the commission, how much would this bill cost you if you bought it at that stated discount rate and a life to maturity of 30 days?

Using the formula, we first determine the cash value of the discount:

$$\frac{30 \text{ days} \times .1522 \times \$10{,}000}{360} = \$126.83$$

Subtracting the discount from the $10,000 face value of the involved bill, the actual cost is $9,837.97. Now you know how to figure out what a bill in the secondary market with less than six months would cost you and what return in terms of discount yield you would earn.

But because you are not using $10,000 to earn the discounted yield, as you would if you had paid $10,000 for a government note or bond with a coupon or interest rate reward, it is proper to convert T-bill yield to its "coupon equivalent" yield.

If you refer to the IMM table, you will see that a 15%, 91-day T-bill actually yields 15.808 if related to its coupon equivalent. In other words, if you simply look at the second column in the table on the horizontal line beginning with "15.00," you'll find that a 15% T-bill discount is equal to a 15.808 equivalent coupon yield. If you don't want to resort to a table but would prefer to play with the calculator, the formula you use is:

$$\frac{\text{Discount}}{\text{Price}} \times \frac{365}{\text{Days to maturity}} = \text{Coupon yield equivalent}$$

(Note that in T-bill discount formulas we always use 360 days, but in calculating the coupon equivalent we always use 365 days to represent a single year.)

Working the coupon-equivalent yield on our 91-day bill at a 15% discount we find:

$$\frac{379.167}{9620.83} \times \frac{365}{91} = 15.808\%$$

How do you calculate six-month (26-week) bills? Use the same formula as for the 90-day bill, but double the discount amount, insert an adjusted cost ($10,000 face minus the doubled discount), double the days to maturity from 91 to 182, and work out as follows:

$$\frac{758.33}{9241.77} \times \frac{365}{182} = 16.456\%$$

If you purchased a 26-week T-bill at auction or through a bank or broker at a stated discount of 15%, you could use the $758.33 to earn compounded daily dividends in a money fund and increase your total yield on the $10,000 while waiting for the bill to mature.

Compound Interest Power

All the earnings derived from money market instruments are, as mentioned, simple interest. None of the investments of a debt nature in the money market offer you the power of compounding. Thus if you invest in CDs for $100,000 or any other interest-bearing instruments in the money market, you'll get your principal back and the interest payable at maturity. Now you have to reinvest that money in order to make it grow and do more work for you.

For example, as we've seen, an investment of $100,000 in a money market instrument at 18% a year, but for 30 days, earns $1,500. To achieve the *annual* simple interest rate of 18%, the $100,000 would have to be rolled over on the maturity of the debt into another investment offering the same annual rate for another 30 days. (You probably wouldn't be able to get the same rate for longer periods.) Then at the end of that investment, you effect another roll-over at the 18% rate. And if you managed to do this twelve times a year you could earn $18,000 on your low-risk investment of $100,000.

But suppose at the end of the first month you could reinvest the principal plus the interest for the next month. Then you would be earning interest not on $100,000 but on $101,500. And at the end of the second month you would be earning 18% annualized interest not on $101,500 but on $103,000. Right?

Wrong.

Because of the power of money working for you through compound interest, where money earns money on the money earned the month before, the day before, or the year before (depending upon how often the compounding period is), you would have in the example above at the end of the second month not $103,000, but $103,-022.50. The $1,500 interest earned at the end of the first month has earned you $22.50 during the second month. And at the end of the third month, which had $103,-022.50 working for you at the 18% annual rate, the dollar amount in your account would have been $104,557.94.

Breaking this down into daily return, the following table indicates the power of compounding on the monthly investment described:

The Power of Compounding

Month	*Investment*	*Monthly yield daily return*	*Month end value (30 days)*
1.	$100,000	$50.00	$101,500
2.	$101,500	$50.75	$103,022.50
3.	$103,022	$51.51	$104,557.94

Naturally, you can use this same method to calculate the money growth of any sum, whether it's $100,000 or $1,-000 or $100. The compound interest rule involves: (a) the frequency of the compounding; (b) the rate of interest stated; (c) the length of time the principal is left to compound; and (d) the amount of money in the principal.

But in the money market it takes millions of dollars each day to be able to achieve compounding power on investments. That is why for sums under $1 million it makes sense to let the money funds compound your money daily.

To save you the drudgery of calculating what happens to $1,000 if it's left in a money fund account that is compounded daily, I have worked out the following table:

Compound Interest Daily Credit on $1,000

Interest rate in %	*Cents/day 360 days*	*Cents/day 365 days*
10% per annum	28¢	27¢
11	31	30
12	33	33
13	36	36
14	39	38
15	42	41
16	44	44
17	47	46
18	50	49
19	53	52
20	56	55

NOTE: Figures in table rounded off for convenience. If you had $1,000 (1,000 shares) on deposit in a money fund on the first of the month and the average yield was 17%, the number of shares at the end of the month would be 1,014.

Using this table you can quickly calculate, for instance, that if you have $5,000 in a money fund paying 16% for a specific 30-day period—and you have not made any additions or withdrawals during the month—the interest you would receive in the form of dividends that buy more shares would be $66.

How did I figure this out?

Simply by multiplying the number of days of compounding (30) by the 44¢-a-day figure in the table for the 16% rate, and then by the amount of $1,000 units (5):

$$30 \text{ days} \times .44 \times 5 = \$66$$

The power of compounding becomes awesome if money is left to accumulate for long periods of time. But investors who move their money in and out of a fund after only one month are obviously not getting the full benefits of compounding, since for brief periods like a month or a week the advantage of compound interest over simple interest is almost negligible. Here is a simplified illustration of the difference in one year between simple interest and compound interest:

Simple Versus Compound Interest

Simple annual interest rate	*Rate if interest is compounded daily*
12%	12.75%
16	17
18	19.125
20	21.25

NOTE: This table covers only a one-year term of interest payments. Money at simple 20% interest for five years would double itself; but this is equivalent to only 14.4% compounded.

There is, of course, an academic approach to compound interest, and I would be remiss if I didn't supply you with the formula:

$$S = A\ (1 + i)^n$$

This formula reveals the amount of money (S) an investment (A) will grow to as it earns interest at the rate of i after n compounding periods. If this formula is employed, you normally would use a table that lists the compound factor $(1 + i)^n$ under varying percentages.

But the lazy way—that is, Sarnoff's way—is to simply refer to the sixth edition of *Financial Compound Interest and Annuity Tables.** Of course, if the compound interest you will receive from money fund investments falls within the limits of my table, then you can save time and money by using it in my practical approach to calculating compound daily interest for a single month.

The final bit of money market math I will cover involves methods of estimating when you will double your money at any given compounded interest rate.

---

* Publication 376, available from Financial Publishing Company, 82 Brookline Ave., Boston, Mass. 02215—a tax-deductible $40 per copy for 2,113 pages of tables and explanatory material.

Double Your Money Estimation

As mentioned above, money at simple 20% interest doubles in five years, but this is equivalent to earning 14.4% compounded. I found this comparison by dividing the magic compound interest number 72 by the number of years it took money at 20% simple interest to double, or 5. Taking my hand calculator I divided 72 by 5 and got 14.4.

This is the rate at which compounded funds will double, whether the amount is $10 or $100,000. Of course, the magic number is not my invention. Many years ago, when banks and thrifts decided to compound savings accounts quarterly, it was determined that to find out how long it took for compounded money to double all you had to do was divide 72 by the stated rate of interest. At 6%, therefore, it takes 12 years to double your money, and at 12 percent, only 6 years, and so on.

The usefulness of this information is that it provides a quick method for assessing the merits of any advertisement offering seemingly generous simple interest on a per annum basis. To do this, divide 72 by the number of years it will take simple interest to double your money and you'll determine whether the simple interest offering is better than a compounded one you may already be invested in.

On the other hand you may notice that some money funds advertise a seven-day yield that at this writing approximates 17.8%. When I asked my son, "How many years would you need to double your money at 17.8%," he immediately shot back, "Four years." How did he know this so fast? He explained that 17.8 was practically 18, and 18 went into 72 four times. When I checked this on the calculator I got 4.04 years. Had I rounded off, as I usually do, I would have arrived at my son's answer instantly.

Money Market Interest Realities

The trouble is that the interest thrown off by money market debt instruments is normally subject to market conditions and therefore may change rapidly and radically. This has been especially true since October 1979, when the Federal Reserve Bank altered its policy with respect to managing the money supply. That is why there can be no guarantee that money market interest rates and discounts will remain within a stable range for any particular period of time during a single month, let alone a year. Here is a graphic illustration of prime rate changes for 1980–1981:

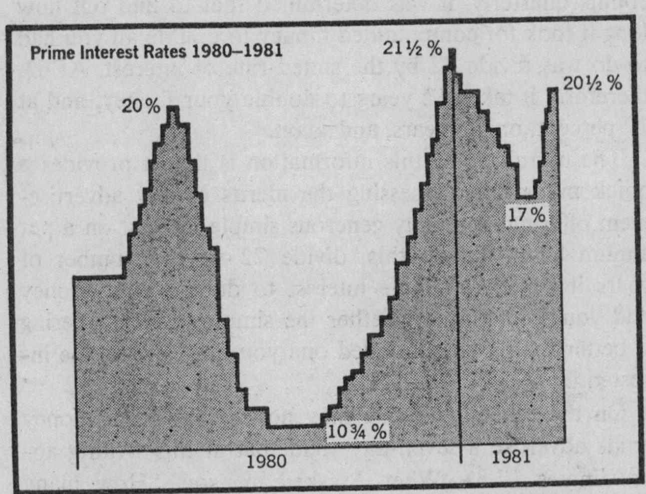

NOTE: This chart is reproduced courtesy of Lone Star Industries.

Since the prime rate traditionally has set the tone for business borrowings from commercial banks, and since the prime is subject to great fluctuations, you cannot expect either money market debt securities or money funds to double your money at any advertised rate or time period. In 1980 the prime rate changed 48 times. During the first half of 1981 it changed 37 times. If you refer to the preceding graph you'll see that the rate rose and fell between a low of ten and three quarters percent and a high of 21½%. How many times will the prime rate change in 1982 or 1983?

Bernard Baruch, when asked what stocks would do, answered succinctly, "They'll fluctuate." People involved in money market transactions know that interest rates will fluctuate, and their ability to forecast changes reasonably separates the men from the boys.

So let's take a look at some interest rate forecasting "secrets."

5
What You Should Know About Interest Rates

It takes only one quick look at the graph on page 73 to realize that interest rates from 1970 to 1980 have had violent ups and downs.

Notice that T-bills never went higher than 10% during this decade until the last quarter of 1979, when, in October, the Federal Reserve Board began its attempt to ride herd on the money supply with interest-related maneuvers. Notice also that rates declined sharply during the three recession periods, 1970-1971, 1974-1975, and 1980. The first rather obvious "secret," then, about interest rates is that when they get high enough and we go into a recession, the condition becomes politically unpalatable to the White House and rates somehow come down sharply to help us out of that recession. See the graph on page 74.

The graph on page 75 reflects the action of short-term interest rates for the second quarter of 1981. Notice that the yield of three-month T-bills during this period never dropped below 14% and went as high as almost 17%. Can it be that interest rates are approaching a peak? If Fed monetary policy helps cause a recession in the last quarter of 1981, chances are that rates will topple sharply as pressure comes from the White House to get us out of a recession. High interest rates have hurt America's two major industries, auto manufacture and housing con-

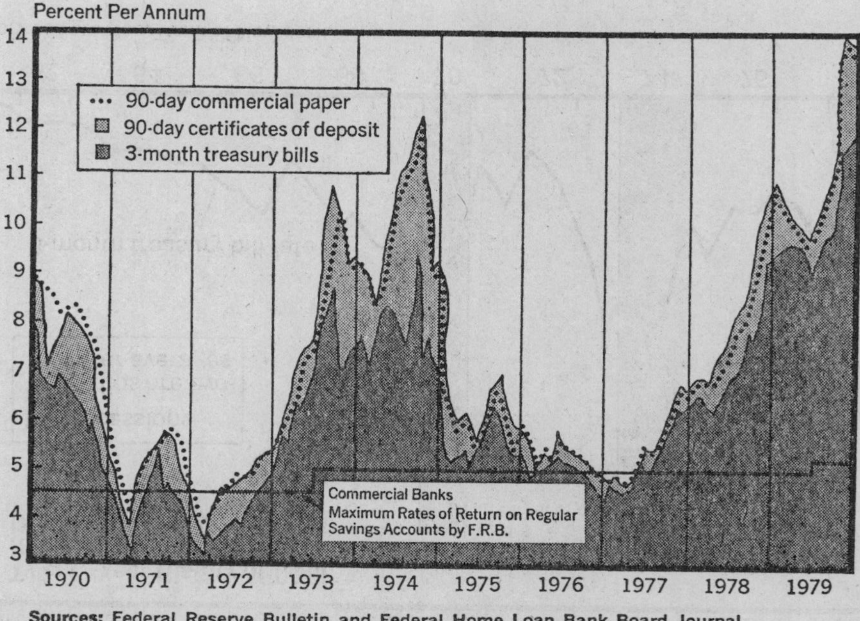

Sources: Federal Reserve Bulletin and Federal Home Loan Bank Board Journal.
Reprinted courtesy of IDS Cash Fund.

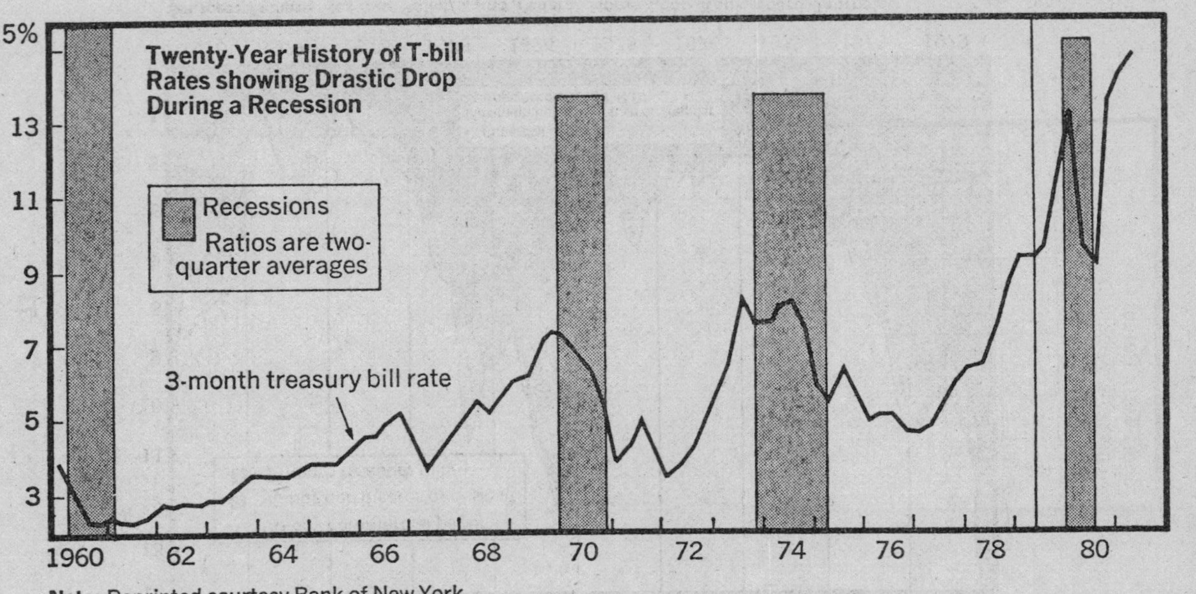

Note: Reprinted courtesy Bank of New York.

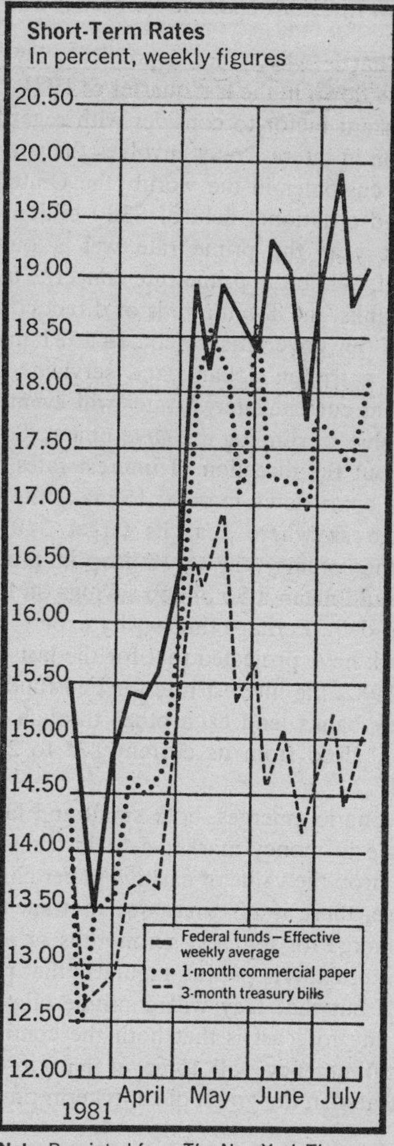

Note: Reprinted from *The New York Times,* July 27, 1981.

struction. That is why, from a political viewpoint, rates have to come down in the last quarter of 1981.

An important factor to consider with regard to the future direction in interest rates involves the cost to the biggest money customer in the world: the United States. In 1970 we had a national debt of $380 billion, and at the end of that year the prime rate was a quarter of its present level. While the prime rate concerns business customers of banks, the T-bill rate is of direct concern to the managers of our government debt. In 1981 that debt is in the area of a trillion dollars; and servicing government borrowings at current interest rates will eventually be the biggest expense of running the government. So the second "secret" about the direction of interest rates is that they will have to come down in order to make the budget estimate emerge anywhere near its target $40-odd billion deficit for the coming year. A 1% drop in T-bill rates, for example, could mean a $6 billion savings on financing the government debt. Perhaps this is why experts at the Bank of New York have projected that for the last half of 1981 and all of 1982, the interest rate for Fed funds (the overnight money banks lend each other through the Reserve System) will drop from its current 17% to 20% levels to 14% to 16%.

If this scenario emerges, both small and large fortunes will be made in money market debt instruments because when rates drop the value of existing paper climbs.

Of course, there is no guarantee that such a rate pattern will emerge for the next six months or a year. Some money market experts predict regularly that rates will not drop at all, but that they will continue climbing to new highs. But my forecast is that both the coming recession and political urgency will force a sharp reverse in the trend illustrated in the graph of short-term rates.

Rates and Inflation

Just a decade ago, in July 1971, there was growing concern about the rising rate of inflation as interest rates began to move higher. The prime rate ran up to 5½%; the discount rate (the rate at which the reserve system lends temporary funds to banks) rose to 4¾%; and good commercial paper traded at 5⅞%. The less risky promises to pay in the form of CDs went for 5¼% for 30 to 59 days. And Fed funds went at 5⅜%. Believe it or not, there was almost universal grumbling among the economic experts that interest rates were too high.

In response to this, Dr. Arthur Burns, the Federal Reserve chairman, blustered through his ever present pipe: "The growth of the money supnly is much too high . . . I can assure you it is not going to last indefinitely."

This reaction of the Reserve Bank translated into higher interest rates because of a fear that inflation—at that time about 4% a year—would get worse.

And it did.

By the fall of 1979 the official inflation rate had risen to 13.5%, and many believed it was actually much higher. The intolerable side effects of such inflation notwithstanding, the Federal Reserve decided in October 1979 to attempt to manage monetary growth by influencing interest rates weekly. Thus, if the money supply expanded too rapidly, it became almost certain that rates would rise for that week; if the money supply fell there was almost an equal certainty that rates would come down a bit from the previous week's levels.

After 22 months of Federal Reserve Bank activity in the money market in pursuit of its altered policy of controlling the money supply, what has happened? The same thing that has happened during the past decade to the cost of a hot dog, taxi ride, movie admission, and just about everything else. We have had an inexorably rising inflation—and the cost of money has gone with the tide. Here is a table showing what has happened to the key rates that concern our very existence in the past ten years.

Key Rates As of July 28, 1981

Key Rate	*Increase since 1971*
Prime rate (on loans to best bank customers)	282%
Federal funds (loans between banks)	235%
Discount rate (loans to banks by the Fed)	195%
Commercial paper (unsecured notes)	204%
Certificates of deposit (new bank paper)	235%

NOTE: The average of the five key rates above represents an increase since 1971 of 230%.

By nature, training, and experience I am a percentage person. Just looking at numbers and noting that they have changed may be meaningless unless we relate the change to percentages in order to see the degree of change. For example, in 1971, a hot dog was still 25¢ in most places I used to pass on the way home from work. Today, probably with less meat and more adulteration, it goes for 85¢ on a street corner in New York, a rise in the decade of 240%, or just about the same advance as the cost of money, which is interest. Using 20/20 hindsight, it is relatively easy for any analyst or even an amateur to track accurately where money rates have been in the past and how they have risen and fallen over a certain period. The real magic is involved when the examiner of past interest rates can come up with a reasonably accurate forecast where rates will be next week, next month, or next year.

In other words, the forecaster has to come up with a reasonably accurate system of interest-rate projections.

But alas—as is the case in any stock or commodity trading system—no one has yet invented such a reliable system of interest-rate projections because prices are not made in the pits or on exchange floors by computers. They're made by people. Whether it's the Wharton School or Salomon Brothers, interest rates on money cannot be accurately forecast by computerized systems because the volatility and direction of these rates depends on too many variables including people.

Still, millions of dollars are expended annually in searching, researching, developing, and undoing computer systems based upon traditional monetary yardsticks. To illustrate what goes into some of these systems, let me use a fictional but typical analyst.

Econometric Parameters

This analyst, whom we'll call Bernie, forms parameters (mathematical constants) for his system by watching a host of acronyms: GNP (Gross National Product), CPI (Consumer Price Index), PPI (Producer Price Index), WPI (Wholesale Price Index), among others. In addition to noting changes in these economic indicators, he examines changes in the GNP Deflator, housing starts, auto sales and auto production, all the key interest rates, and the Money Supply. He reads omnivorously most of the leading publications of money center banks, such as Chase, Citibank, Morgan, Bank of New York, and the money market publications of stockbrokers, such as Hutton's *Money Market Tactician*. Throughout the day he has one eye glued to wire services such as Reuters, Telerate, Dow-Jones, Commodity News Services, and any other reliable sources that broadcast financial information on wires or terminal display screens.

Moreover, Bernie is in touch with friends at the Fed, with economists and econometricians at universities and with the same type of experts at the Wharton School Data Bank and the Conference Board. He also has telephone liaison with experts at the big money banks, stockbrokerage houses, and financial firms dealing in money market instruments.

It takes a lot of time and energy for Bernie to keep up with the factors that influence interest-rate direction and to apply the information properly to fine-tuned computerized systems. Are Bernie's forecasts usually accurate? Sometimes they are, and sometimes they're dead wrong. But the reason his firm spends the millions of dollars a year required to receive all this information and maintain an interest-forecasting computer program is that Bernie turns out to be right more times than he is wrong.

Sarnoff's Secrets

I almost completely disregard the economic acronyms spewed out each month by government agencies. The statistics and the traditional yardsticks have become so distorted over the years since President Eisenhower's administration by elimination and inclusion of data that for me they have completely lost credibility. Evidently I am not completely alone in this line of thinking. A friend out West who is investment manager for the largest company in its industry calls these government yardsticks "financial cosmetics" designed to make it possible for the administration always to present its best financial face to the public—even though that face may in reality be ravaged and wrinkled.

The biggest laugh I got from these figures came in 1981, when the government announced that the "official" inflation rate had dropped to 8½%. On the same day this triumphant event was announced by government spokespeople, I saw a clerk in the local supermarket diligently stamping tuna fish cans over with a higher price. The price had gone from $1.19 a can to $1.39, an increase over the previous day of 16.8%. On the way home I stopped at a local dairy store and bought a half-gallon of milk for $1.15, when a few days before it had been 99¢, an increase of 20.2%. After I got home I went to our larder and fished out a can of the same brand of tuna, bought the previous year for 69¢; thus my latest purchase of tuna at $1.39 represented an increase in cost of 101% for the year. Of course, one must assume that the price of tuna fish was not a very important part of the official calculations of inflation. But lots of little items like that affect the consumer's pocketbook directly.

So if I don't rely on customary government statistics for my own interest-rate forecasts, how can I possibly arrive at any accurate predictions? The government used to help me tremendously, but in a rather unusual way. *I used to read what its spokespeople had to say about interest rates and predict the opposite.*

For example, in the summer of 1978, both the secretary of the treasury and the secretary of commerce assured one and all that interest rates (the prime was then about 8%) would decline drastically. While no timetable was presented with these predictions, the implication was that the drop would come in the fall.

Shortly after these governmental forecasts were aired in the media, an economist whose trenchant observations had become popular at various banking and business conferences came out with the assertion that the prime rate would not decline but would instead rise to at least 9½% in 1978. If the chief economist for the Harris Bank in Chicago could predict that interest rates would rise even though experts in public positions had stated they would fall, whom would I rather believe?

So I predicted that rates would *absolutely* rise. And they did. From that time until Mr. Reagan took the oath of office in January 1981, I was able to forecast rate direction fairly accurately by simply assuming the opposite of Washington's pronouncements on the subject.

I now follow closely the price differences from month to month in the trading of financial futures contracts.* In these volatile markets, contracts to buy or sell T-bills, T-bonds, CDs and commercial paper are traded on exchanges for future delivery during designated months. The narrowing or widening of the differences between the trading months indicates what professionals think will happen to rates. (Listings of prices of financial futures and the months traded are to be found in the financial sections of major newspapers.) In addition, I monitor the differences between delivery months in gold, silver, platinum, and copper futures because these differences sometimes serve as a beacon to interest-rate change and direction.

Interest Rate Strategies

Assuming that you are able to obtain reasonably reliable advance notice of interest-rate changes, how can you profit from this information?

You can dispose of short-term money market instruments and buy long-term debt. If rates go down, the values of your long-term notes and bonds will adjust themselves quickly in the marketplace and you will reap handsome profits on low risk. If rates do not decline, but instead keep rising, and your investment decision has been wrong, dispose of the long-term securities and switch back to short-term.

If you do not want to assume the risk that goes with investment in debt instruments that change in price as inter-

* You can receive detailed information about financial futures without charge or obligation by writing the author c/o the publisher.

est rates change, you can lock up funds for six months to two-and-a-half years at historically high rates in bank or thrift certificates. This can be done with as little as $1,000.

When it comes to the billions of dollars invested in money funds, the level of interest rates and their changes are of utmost importance to the investment advisers managing the portfolios. Most of the money funds have already performed excellently in rising interest rate markets. But how will they perform during long periods of interest-rate decline?

To find some clues to this answer, let's do some simple money fund portfolio analysis.

6

Analyzing and Rating the Money Funds

At some point during the exciting Shearson TV commercial, which assures listeners that that brokerage firm has all the answers to money questions, a bespectacled, professorial-looking actor poses the question, "How do I know what's right for me?"

The answer, of course, is not the one aired on TV. You can't expect Shearson, Merrill Lynch, Hutton, Bache, Donoghue, Sarnoff, or anyone else to make your own financial decisions. Only *you* can provide the answer. You should be as concerned and knowledgeable about your investment objectives as you are about your career goals.

And if you want to invest in money funds, the question becomes, How can you best analyze the money fund portfolios in order to select the funds that fit your own objectives and needs?

Once you have set your personal goals and determined your specific needs, the two major factors that may make one money fund better for you than another are safety and yield. Bill Donoghue developed what he calls his SLY system, "stressing Safety, Liquidity and Yield." This is the philosophy behind his 24-issue-a-year *Moneyletter*, which includes such advice as "Ten Pitfalls to Avoid in the

Money Market" and "The Ten Best Deals in The Money Market."*

But of most value in attempting to analyze both the performance (the percentage payout per share), or yield, and the safety of the funds in accordance with what percentage of the investments is allocated to money market debt instruments of varying risks is Donoghue's weekly *Money Fund Report*.† The listings from the July 13, 1981, issue are reproduced in the following table:

---

* Donoghue's *Moneyletter* currently sells for 87 tax-deductible dollars a year. You may want to prepay the subscription, since you would then automatically receive two editions of Donoghue's *Money Fund Directory* (updated twice a year and selling for 12 tax-deductible dollars each).

† A year's subscription (50 weeks) costs $260.

Monday, July 13, 1981

ISSN#0197-7091 Assets are up $2.6 billion. Average maturity shortened 2 days, reversing a 4-week trend of lengthening maturities, tying in with the unusually high ($81.5 billion) amount of 6-month MMCs due to mature in July. WELCOME: Securities Group Money Fund & Sentry Cash Management!! #291

			Investment results					Portfolio holdings (%)								
			For period ended: 7/8/81			12-Mo.		U.S.								
Net assets ($ mill)	Fund	Valuation method	7-Day	30-Day	30 day mo ago	YTD as of 5/31	Avg. mat. (days)	Treas.	Other	Repos	CDs	Banker's accept	Comm'l paper	Euro$, CDs, TDs	Yankee$, CDs, BAs	Other
	GENERAL PURPOSE															
$ 238.7	American General	3	17.9	17.2	16.8	13.4	15	—	—	12	—	—	88	—	—	—
297.3	American Liquid Trust	1	16.7	16.8	16.3	12.8	25	—	—	3	58	39	—	—	—	—
48.9	Babson Money Mkt	3	16.9	16.9	16.4	12.9	26	—	—	—	—	28	72	—	—	—
161.0	Boston Company Cash Mgt	4	17.3	17.4	16.5	12.4	19	—	3	6	3	—	88	—	—	—
1,118.7	Capital Preservation	1	17.7	17.0	15.2	11.9	9	58	—	42m	—	—	—	—	—	—
351.8	Capital Preservation Fund II	1	18.9	18.4	17.0	12.5	2	—	—	100m	—	—	—	—	—	—
175.9	Cardinal Government Secs.	1	16.4	16.8	16.3	—	9	—	91	9	—	—	—	—	—	—
514.9	Cash Mgmt Trust	1	17.9	17.8	17.3	12.5	13	—	—	24	13	3	42	—	18	—
56.7	Centennial Cash Mgmt.	1	17.2	17.5	15.6	12.5	16	—	—	16	—	—	84	—	—	—
7.3	Colonial Money Mkt Tr. k	4	16.7	16.7	16.5	—	31	4	15	12	8	3	58	—	—	—
674.4	Columbia Daily Income	1	17.1	16.8	15.4	12.6	24	—	—	10	—	30	60	—	—	—
1,372.4	Delaware Cash Reserves	4	17.8	17.6	17.2	13.1	29	—	—	—	14	17	35	6	28	—

53.6	Dollar Reserves	3	17.9	18.3	17.8	—	14	—	—	17	—	12	66	5	—	—
6,161.0	Dreyfus Liquid Assets	4	17.3	17.1	16.3	12.8	28	—	1	—	35	6	20	38	—	—
203.8	Eaton & Howard Cash	3	17.1	17.4	16.6	12.8	24	—	—	—	24	4	72	—	—	—
187.0	Equitable Money Mkt Acct	4	16.6	16.7	15.8	—	26	—	—	—	23	10	43	24	—	—
19.5	FBL Money Mkt Fund n	1	16.3	17.2	17.2	—	23	—	—	3	3	—	94	—	—	—
2,201.8	Fidelity Cash Reserves	4	17.1	17.2	16.6	12.9	28	—	2	—	7	—	18	37	36	—
3,363.3	Fidelity Daily Income	4	16.6	16.8	16.1	12.8	31	—	2	4	43	28	23	—	—	—
235.1	Financial Daily Income	2	17.8	17.9	17.4	13.3	13	—	1	—	—	—	99	—	—	—
446.1	First Investors Cash Mgt	1	17.3	17.4	16.7	13.1	24	—	—	1	73	15	11	—	—	—
820.8	First Variable Rate	1	16.9	16.5	16.1	12.8	34b	9	32	59	—	—	—	—	—	—
3.4	Florida Mutual US Govt. k	4	15.1	15.1	14.9	—	20	29	42	29m	—	—	—	—	—	—
726.9	Franklin Money Fund	1	17.1	16.9	16.6	13.0	17	—	—	11	24	42	23	—	—	—
46.3	Franklin Federal M.F.	1	17.3	15.6	14.1	12.1	3	11	—	89	—	—	—	—	—	—
707.4	Fund/Govt. Investors	4	17.4	17.3	17.0	12.1	7	27	73	—	—	—	—	—	—	—
1.1	Fund/Ready Income	4	14.2	17.7	15.1	—	46L	60	40	—	—	—	—	—	—	—
297.1	Government Investors Trust	1	17.4	17.2	16.7	13.1	24	—	13	87	—	—	—	—	—	—
828.2	IDS Cash Mgt	3	16.9	17.0	16.4	13.1	32	—	2	—	16	26	51	5	—	—
366.3	John Hancock Cash Mgt	4	16.7	16.9	16.5	12.7	29	—	—	—	12	8	68	—	12	—
2,021.3	Kemper Money Market	3	17.4	17.2	15.8	13.2	30	—	—	—	—	—	61	26	13	—
178.2	Lexington Money Market	1	17.5	17.7	17.2	12.7	23	—	—	—	2	5	90	—	3	—
44.4	Liquid Green Trust	4	17.4	17.3	17.0	—	24	—	—	11	17	13	39	—	20	—
302.7	Lord Abbett Cash Reserve	3	17.2	17.2	16.7	12.7	30	—	4	—	40	10	46	—	—	—
517.6	Lutheran Brthd M. M. n	4	16.7	16.2	15.4	13.1	29	—	—	—	11	3	60	15	—	11
222.0	MIF/Nationwide M.M. n	3	16.7	16.6	16.0	12.6	35	4	—	—	8	44	44	—	—	—
655.3	Mass Cash Mgt Trust	1	17.6	17.3	16.4	12.4	25	—	—	—	4	3	75	18	—	—
177.4	Midwest Income ST Govt.	4	16.3	16.2	15.7	11.9	30	3	64	33m	—	—	—	—	—	—
409.6	Money Market Mgt	4	16.6	16.2	15.1	12.5	29	—	—	—	15	10	52	11	—	12
18.3	Money Shares. Inc.	3	15.3	15.9	15.6	12.0	18	64	—	—	—	—	36	—	—	—
309.0	Mutual of Omaha	4	17.3	17.5	17.1	13.0	22	—	4	1	3	2	81	8	—	1

Net assets ($ mill)	Fund	Valuation method	Investment results: For period ended: 7/8/81 7-Day	30-Day	30 day mo ago	12-Mo. YTD as of 5/31	Avg. mat. (days)	Portfolio holdings (%): U.S. Treas.	U.S. Other	Repos	CDs	Banker's accept	Comm'l paper	Euro$, CDs, TDs	Yankee$, CDs, BAs	Other
457.3	NEL Cash Mgt. Trust	4	17.4	17.3	16.4	12.7	25	—	—	—	9	12	55	24	—	—
1,910.2	NRTA-AARP US Gv MMTr	4	16.1	15.7	15.0	12.5	33	1	80	19	—	—	—	—	—	—
19.8	Phoenix-Chase M.M. Series	4	17.9	17.9	17.6	—	15	—	—	—	—	11	68	13	8	—
36.2	Plimoney Fund, Inc.	1	16.7	16.7	16.2	12.4	33	—	—	12	39	—	32	14	3	—
2.9	Principal Protection Govt.	4	18.2	16.7	16.4	—	1 S	—	—	100m	—	—	—	—	—	—
305.1	Putnam Daily Div Trust	4	17.0	17.1	16.3	12.6	37	—	—	6	20	20	15	33	6	—
2,910.7	Reserve	4	17.5	17.5	16.9	13.1	17	—	1	7	12	1	—	72	—	7
145.5	St. Paul Money Fund, Inc.	3	17.1	17.4	17.6	12.8	21	—	—	—	6	1	93	—	—	—
990.8	Scudder Cash Inv Trust	3	17.1	17.3	17.2	13.0	20	—	3	—	32	13	52	—	—	—
.9	Securities Group M.F.	1	17.8	—	—	—	8	100	—	—	—	—	—	—	—	—
59.9	Security Cash Fund	4	16.2	16.6	16.3	—	23	—	—	7	—	—	93	—	—	—
57.8	Selected Money Market	4	16.8	17.0	16.1	12.7	28	—	—	—	7	23	56	—	14	—
16.0	Sentry Cash Mgmt.	4	17.1	17.3	—	—	24	4	—	—	—	9	87	—	—	—
98.6	Short-Term Yield Securities	1	17.3	17.3	16.5	12.7	14	—	—	9	5	—	86	—	—	—
9.4	Sigma Money Market Fund	3	16.7	17.0	—	—	7	—	3	—	—	—	97	—	—	—
4.0	Steadman Federal Securities	4	14.0	13.9	12.9	—	18	23	14	63	—	—	—	—	—	—
636.0	SteinRoe Cash Reserves	3	17.1	17.1	16.2	12.9	20	—	—	1	9	8	59	23	—	—
2,481.1	T. Rowe Price Prime Res	2*	17.6	17.4	16.4	13.3	23	—	—	7	6	1	43	21	22	—
3.2	Texas Money Fund	3	17.4	17.8	17.6	—	40	—	29	14	13	—	44	—	—	—

191.9	Transamerica Cash Reserves	4	17.1	17.0	16.6	—	25	—	3	4	15	8	44	—	—	26
60.3	USAA Mutual M.M. Fund	4	16.8	16.9	16.7	—	28	—	—	—	15	15	70	—	—	—
649.4	Union Cash Mgt., Inc.	2	17.5	17.6	17.2	13.6	18	—	—	—	—	—	11	49	40	—
345.6	United Cash Management	2	17.6	17.6	16.7	13.0	19	—	—	—	1	1	81	—	17	—
264.6	Value Line Cash	1	17.9	18.1	17.3	13.6	22	—	—	—	—	—	100	—	—	—
768.0	Vanguard Money Mkt Trust	3	17.3	17.6	17.2	12.9	27	—	—	6	10	12	72	—	—	—
$ 38,967.7	Average Yield		17.04	17.05	16.38	12.77										
	STOCKBROKER/GENERAL PURPOSE															
$ 1,333.0	Alliance Capital Reserves	3	16.9	17.0	16.4	12.7	26	—	—	—	20	12	68	—	—	—
72.6	Alliance Government Res	3	15.9	16.4	15.7	11.8	23	9	91	—	—	—	—	—	—	—
85.7	BIRR Wilson Money Fund	1	18.0	17.7	17.1	—	17	—	—	5	15	54	26	—	—	—
43.6	Carnegie Gov't Securities	1	16.4	16.8	16.6	12.4	9	1	88	11	—	—	—	—	—	—
2,585.2	Cash Equivalent Fund	3	17.8	17.4	15.7	13.2	27	—	—	—	—	—	67	21	12	—
5,451.3	Cash Reserve Mgt	1	17.0	17.5	17.4	13.1	26	—	1	1	6	3	74	15	—	—
223.8	Composite Cash Mgt Co.	1	17.4	17.5	16.2	12.9	27	—	4	2	11	2	64	—	17	—
1,112.0	Current Interest	3	17.1	17.2	16.5	12.5	25	—	—	—	14	8	78	—	—	—
689.8	DBL Cash Fund	4	16.8	16.8	16.6	—	28	—	3	—	11	7	65	14	—	—
4,185.6	Daily Cash Accumulation	3	17.6	17.5	16.7	13.1	27	3	—	—	13	2	71	9	—	2a
680.7	Daily Income	3	16.4	16.4	16.5	12.5	33	—	18	4	40	—	37	—	—	1
441.1	ED Jones Dly Passport	4	16.6	16.0	14.9	12.6	29	—	—	5	10	7	52	14	—	12
532.5	Gradison Cash Reserves	4	17.1	17.1	16.0	12.7	26	—	1	1	12	21	65	—	—	—
474.8	INA Cash Fund, Inc.	3**	17.3	17.3	16.6	12.7	27	—	—	—	14	5	73	8	—	—
7,263.7	InterCapital Liquid Asset	4	16.8	16.7	16.1	12.9	29	1	—	—	46	—	53	—	—	—
227.4	Legg Mason Cash Res Trust	4	16.7	16.3	15.4	12.8	26	—	—	31	16	5	71	—	—	5
167.8	Lehman Cash Mgt., Inc.	2	17.8	17.7	17.5	—	18	—	—	—	—	—	43	34	23	—
1,703.5	Liquid Capital Income	4	17.1	17.2	17.0	12.9	23	—	17	3	24	6	12	—	—	38
119.3	McDonald Money Market	4	17.3	17.4	—	—	15	—	—	4	32	28	11	25	—	—

Net assets ($ mill)	Fund	Valuation method	Investment results: For period ended: 7/8/81 7-Day	30-Day	30 day mo ago	12-Mo. YTD as of 5/31	Avg. mat. (days)	Portfolio holdings (%): U.S. Treas.	U.S. Other	Repos	CDs	Banker's accept	Comm'l paper	Euro$, CDs, TDs	Yankee$, CDs, BAs	Other
	Merrill Lynch															
7,800.2	CMA Money Trust	1	15.6	16.5	16.6	12.4	29	14	—	—	45	13	28	—	—	—
283.0	Merrill Lynch Govt	3	16.3	16.5	16.4	12.4	16	50	—	50m	—	—	—	—	—	—
17,735.5	Merrill Lynch Ready	1	15.9	16.6	16.8	12.3	31	26	—	7	39	8	20	—	—	—
3,048.0	MoneyMart Assets	1	17.7	17.4	16.5	13.0	24	—	—	3	22	5	46	24	—	—
54.6	Morgan Keegan Daily Cash	4	16.8	16.3	14.9	—	24	—	—	10	19	2	46	7	—	16
20.1	Mutual of Omaha Cash	4	16.6	16.9	17.3	—	15	—	—	10	—	—	90	—	—	—
1,698.6	National Liquid Reserves	3	17.1	16.9	16.0	12.8	27	—	—	—	18	5	61	16	—	—
1,301.8	Oppenheimer Money Mkt	3	17.6	17.7	17.0	13.3	23	—	—	—	1	4	95	—	—	—
4,247.8	Paine Webber Cashfund	3	16.6	16.6	16.0	12.7	33	6	4	1	29	20	40	—	—	—
4,084.1	Shearson Daily Dividend, Inc.	4	16.9	16.8	16.2	13.1	29	—	—	—	7	3	14	76	—	—
171.1	Shearson Gov't Agency	4	15.8	15.9	15.0	—	25	9	80	11	—	—	—	—	—	—
250.9	Short Term Income Fund	3	16.6	16.5	16.3	12.4	32	—	12	3	45	—	39	—	—	1
153.5	Trust/Cash Reserves	4	16.6	16.1	15.4	12.5	27	—	—	7	18	4	49	9	—	13
221.6	Tucker Anthony Cash Mgt	4	17.3	17.3	17.2	—	27	—	6	—	—	3	91	—	—	—
967.3	Webster Cash Reserve	3	17.2	17.2	16.6	12.9	26	—	9	—	39	6	33	13	—	—
69,431.5	Average Yield		16.90	16.91	16.34	12.72										

	INSTITUTIONS ONLY															
	Dreyfus Service Corp.															
171.0	Dreyfus Govt Series	4	17.6	16.2	15.1	12.0	2	16	—	84	—	—	—	—	—	—
1,905.0	Dreyfus Money Market	4	17.6	17.5	16.6	12.9	25	1	—	3	38	9	17	32	—	—
	Federated Securities															
3,188.0	Federated Master Trust	4	17.1	17.0	16.2	12.9	22	—	—	2	—	—	93	—	—	5
137.2	Liquid Cash Trust	4	18.2	17.6	17.6	—	1S	—	—	85	—	—	—	—	—	15
1,580.2	Money Market Trust	4	16.5	15.9	14.8	12.7	20	—	—	9	49	30	1	—	—	11
3,581.2	Trust/US Govt Secs	4	16.2	15.8	15.3	12.0	34	10	55	35	—	—	—	—	—	—
1,228.8	Trust/US Treas Obligs.	4	15.6	15.4	15.1	12.1	35	70	—	30	—	—	—	—	—	—
	Fidelity Money Market Trust															
514.6	Domestic	4	17.2	17.1	16.0	12.7	26	—	5	14	21	21	39	—	—	—
541.1	Government	4	17.8	17.5	16.5	12.6	10	—	36	64	—	—	—	—	—	—
64.0	US Treasury	4	18.4	17.8	17.6	—	1S	—	—	100	—	—	—	—	—	—
	Goldman, Sachs & Co.															
750.6	ILA Government	4	16.7	16.6	15.7	12.5	23	7	74	19	—	—	—	—	—	—
2,056.6	ILA Prime Obligations	4	17.4	17.6	17.1	12.7	19	—	—	3	21	5	71	—	—	—
925.5	Mer Lynch Institutional	3	17.0	17.0	16.1	13.0	21	—	1	6m	62	6	25	—	—	—
	Shearson Loeb Rhoades, Inc.															
768.8	FedFund	3	16.6	16.6	15.9	12.3	32	5	66	29	—	—	—	—	—	—
206.0	T-Fund	3	16.4	15.8	15.4	12.5	18	58	—	42	—	—	—	—	—	—
3,150.2	TempFund	3	16.8	16.7	16.1	12.8	32	8	—	8	36	17	31	—	—	—
20,768.8	Average Yield		17.07	16.76	16.07	12.55										
129,168.0	Total Assets—All Funds															
	Average Yield		17.00	16.97	16.32	12.68										
	Average Maturity (wtd by assets)		27	25	27											

All yields reported represent the annualized total return yield net of management fees and expenses. The average maturity figures are dollar weighted for the value of portfolio holdings.

VALUATION METHODS: 1—Constant Net Asset Value, Mark-to-Market. **2**—Variable Net Asset Value, Mark-to-Market. **3**—Constant Net Asset Value, 120-day Maximum Average Maturity (penny rounding): **4**—Amortized Cost, Straight Line Accrual:*—Applied for #3:**—Applied for #4.

NOTES: a—Represents letters of credit: **b**—Average term to next rate adjustment date: **c**—Bonds: **d**—Estimates: **f**—Government guaranteed loan participations. **g**—Includes acceptances of and deposits in full US branches of foreign banks: **h**—Yield reduced by service fee: **k**—Manager absorbing a portion of fund expenses or management fee: **L**—Longest maturity: **m**—US Treasury obligations purchased under repurchase agreements: **n**—This fund charges a $100 one-time new account fee: **n/a**—Not available: **p**—CDs of foreign branches of US banks only: **S**—Shortest maturity:*—Seven-day average not representative of current yield due to effect of varying net asset value.

SUBSCRIPTIONS: Sample Copy free upon request. Write Box 540, 770 Washington St., Holliston, Mass., 01746 or call (617) 429-5930. Subscription price is $260 for 50 issues (one year). Donoghue's *Money Fund Directory*, published Fall and Spring, $12 each. Subscription contract cannot be assigned by publisher without prior consent.

The first column (net assets) gives the size of the fund in millions of dollars. Personally I would avoid investing in any fund under $250 million because I have always felt that bigness is a sign of safety and experience. But I may be totally wrong in this concept. In any event, if I were attracted to a small fund, I'd certainly want to watch for at least four weeks to measure the weekly rate of growth or decline before making a move.

The second column (fund) provides the abbreviated name of the money fund. (See Appendix A for the full name, address, toll-free number, and other data for most of the funds listed in this table.) This column is divided into three sections: general-purpose funds; stockbroker/general purpose; and institutions only.

The third column identifies the valuation methods. There seems to be a definite trend toward methods 3 and 4 and away from 1 and 2. But in reality I don't consider these numbers particularly important in fund selection.

The fourth through seventh columns list investment results for various periods.

The eighth column covers the average maturity of the fund portfolios. This is a very important consideration in both the rating and the purchase of fund shares. If the trend of short-term interest rates keeps rising, the number of days to maturity should shorten. If the trend reverses and rates decline, the average number of days to maturity should lengthen. If highest yield is sought in rising markets, funds with shortest maturities should be contemplated for purchase. In falling markets, shift to funds with lengthening maturities—and then shift out to the shorter ones when rates again reverse and start to rise.

Much of the material in these first eight columns—concerning asset size, average maturity, and weekly and monthly fund yield—appears in condensed form in the following newspapers on the days indicated:

The New York Times (Friday and Sunday)
Chicago Tribune (Friday and Tuesday)
Washington Post (Monday)
Los Angeles Times (Monday)
San Francisco Examiner (Friday)
San Francisco Chronicle (Friday)
Boston Globe (Friday and Sunday)
Detroit News (Tuesday)
Miami News (Friday)
Tallahassee Democrat (Sunday)

But understandably none of these papers provides weekly information regarding what the funds do with the billions of dollars pouring in to them—in other words, what they actually invest in to earn the high dividends paid daily to the investors after expenses.

That's why *columns nine through seventeen* in Donoghue's *Money Fund Report* are invaluable time savers for any analytically minded person—they are at least a guide to the categories of investment if not to the actual debt instruments in the portfolios themselves. To use this information properly, either refer to your own safety rating scale or use the one I supplied in chapter 3, reproduced again below. Remember: lowest number, highest safety.

1. T-bills
2. Other government bonds and notes
3. Government agency obligations
4. Repos
5. Banker's Acceptances
6. Bank certificates of deposit (domestic CDs)
7. Domestic Eurodollar CDs and debt
8. Foreign Eurodollar CDs and debt (including Yankee bonds)
9. Commercial paper and corporate notes

Using this risk yardstick, I examined the funds listed in the *Money Fund Report* and noticed how few of them actually held government securities on July 8 (reporting date of the July 13 *Report*). Check for yourself and see. Yet when I queried a sampling of people who own and invest in money funds, they almost all admitted that they were attracted to the funds because of their dealings in the *safe* government securities markets.

On the other side of the money market seesaw is the predominant position of commercial paper in the diversified portfolios of the "general purpose" and "stockbroker/general purpose" funds. About half of them held more than 50% of their portfolio in corporate paper promises to repay—backed mainly by reputation.

A Practical Method for Money Fund Portfolios Rating

As already pointed out, there are two main ingredients in evaluating any large money market portfolio: (1) safety of committed principal, and (2) yield. Now remembering Donoghue's SLY system, you may rightfully ask, "What about liquidity?" And my answer is that *all* no-load money funds that offer check and expedited redemption (wire and telephone) features are liquid. They also have to be $1-a-share net constant asset value funds and compound dividends daily.

Practically speaking, then, I consider only safety (S) and Yield (Y). I have divided my money fund ratings into four areas for each ingredient as follows:

Safety Ratings	*Yield Ratings*
G (Good)	*G (Good)*
50% or more in governments, BAs, repos, and bank CDs 0% Euro CDs 20% or less prime commercial paper	30-day yield higher than reported 30-day yield for industry

PG (Pretty good) 20%–50% governments, BAs, repos, and bank CDs 0% Euro CDs 40% or less prime commercial paper	*PG (Pretty good)* 30-day yield equal to but not lower than .75% under industry average yield for same 30-day period
R (Risky) 0% governments, BAs, or repos 20% or less CDs 50% or more Euro CDs and commercial paper	*R (Risky)* 30-day yield lower than .75% under industry average yield for same 30-day period, but not more than 1% lower
X (Avoid or switch) 0% governments, BAs, 0% repos and CDs 100% Euro CDs and commercial paper	*X (Avoid or switch)* Yield for 30-day period over 1% lower than industry average for same 30-day period

The almost daily movement of money market securities into and out of large portfolios like money funds can appear to be very confusing. But there is a planned purpose behind when to buy, when (if necessary) to sell, and when to leave the security to mature. And each fund does it in a different manner, shifting with the winds of change in the world's money markets.

For your convenience, I have supplied my own ratings of the leading money funds in Appendix A. These ratings were compiled by applying the preceding method to the data available on July 8, 1981. Obviously, by the time you read this, the portfolios I have rated by my method will have changed in various ways, but the rationale behind my rating system will still apply for you in evaluating any particular fund.

Just remember, when you're rating money funds, to do so on the basis of the factor that means the most to you. Some of my relatives believe Value Line is the best in the money fund game. But I would have to rate it X for safety because on July 8, 1981, the portfolio was 100% invested in commercial paper. On the other hand, from the yield standpoint, Value Line Cash receives my top rating, G, because it performed better than the monthly average.

Using my rating method, note in Donoghue's table that Daily Income contains over 50% of the governments, repos, and CDs that could have given it a G rating, but it also contains 37% commercial paper. So I have arbitrarily rated it PG for safety. Now, what about yield? For the 30-day reported period, Daily Income earned on a gross basis for shareholders 16.4%. The average for that same period turned out to be 16.97%. Thus because Daily Income reported .57% under the average, it gets a PG rating for yield as well.

But is this superficial examination sufficient for anyone, including me, to make a judgment that Daily Income would be better or worse for you than Putnam Daily Dividend Trust or IDS Cash? Or Dreyfus Liquid Assets?

The obvious answer is, indeed, it is not sufficient—but it is a beacon toward a safe harbor whose approach is strewn with shoals. Examining the number of days of the average maturity of Daily Income's portfolio, I noticed that on July 8 it stood at 33 days, a rather long interval compared with other stockbroker/general purpose funds. This indicated to me that the advisors to this fund, Reich & Tang, were operating on the assumption that the near future would bring lower short-term rates. Thus, if rates did go down from midsummer to fall, chances are that this fund would report better yields than those that had shorter maturities on July 8.

To look at the fund in more depth, I decided to examine the kind of securities it held. The Daily Income portfolio as of June 30, 1981, is reproduced in the following table.

Daily Income Fund, Inc. Investments, June 30, 1981 (unaudited)

Face amount (B)		Due date	Interest rates at date of purchase: Stated rate	Interest rates at date of purchase: Annualized yield (C)	Market value (D)
CERTIFICATES OF DEPOSIT (37.4%)					
$ 5,000,000	American Security Bank	8/17/81	17.13%	18.12%	$ 4,996,922
4,000,000	Bank of America	7/14/81	17.15	18.90	4,002,819
5,000,000	Bank of America	8/3/81	18.77	20.49	4,967,160
5,000,000	Bank of America	8/18/81	19.00	20.72	4,977,429
5,000,000	Bank of America	11/2/81	15.75	16.71	4,997,620
7,000,000	Bank of America	12/7/81	16.00	16.88	6,985,013
8,000,000	Crocker National Bank	7/20/81	15.75	16.95	7,993,234
5,000,000	Crocker National Bank	7/20/81	16.40	17.33	4,996,549
5,000,000	Crocker National Bank	9/8/81	15.20	16.01	4,979,251
5,000,000	Crocker National Bank	9/14/81	13.38	14.03	4,959,581
5,000,000	Crocker National Bank	11/16/81	18.15	19.25	5,026,734
5,000,000	Detroit Bank & Trust Co.	7/13/81	17.40	19.13	5,000,481
10,000,000	Detroit Bank & Trust Co.	7/27/81	17.35	19.07	10,001,755
5,000,000	Detroit Bank & Trust Co.	12/28/81	16.10	16.99	5,000,617
6,000,000	First National Bank, Dallas	8/17/81	16.95	17.93	5,994,962
7,000,000	First National Bank, Dallas	8/31/81	16.75	18.10	6,995,832
5,000,000	First National Bank, Dallas	12/15/81	15.40	16.23	4,980,119
10,000,000	Harris Trust & Savings Bank	7/8/81	18.25	20.05	10,002,040
5,000,000	Maryland National Bank	12/15/81	15.90	16.78	4,991,052
10,000,000	Mellon Bank	7/23/81	17.05	18.73	10,000,446

5,000,000	Mellon Bank	11/23/81	17.00	17.99	5,006,722
5,000,000	Morgan Guaranty Trust Co.	7/6/81	17.75	19.58	5,001,194
5,000,000	Morgan Guaranty Trust Co.	7/27/81	17.45	19.20	5,001,248
7,000,000	Morgan Guaranty Trust Co.	9/8/81	16.95	18.33	6,993,940
5,000,000	Morgan Guaranty Trust Co.	9/9/81	16.75	18.10	4,996,913
5,500,000	Morgan Guaranty Trust Co.	9/17/81	17.70	19.20	5,508,171
5,000,000	Morgan Guaranty Trust Co.	9/24/81	16.70	18.06	5,001,344
7,000,000	National Bank, Detroit	7/21/81	18.80	20.65	7,006,016
5,000,000	National Bank, Detroit	7/24/81	17.75	19.53	5,001,965
5,000,000	National Bank, Detroit	7/29/81	17.40	19.13	5,001,151
5,000,000	National City Bank, Cleveland	9/14/81	17.00	18.36	4,999,139
7,000,000	Northern Trust Co.	8/14/81	16.50	17.94	6,994,606
7,000,000	Northern Trust Co.	8/17/81	16.50	17.93	6,994,282
10,000,000	Northwestern National Bank, Minneapolis	7/27/81	17.85	19.51	10,004,470
5,000,000	Pittsburgh National Bank	7/7/81	14.88	15.65	4,997,636
5,000,000	Pittsburgh National Bank	7/16/81	16.50	17.45	4,985,432
10,000,000	Pittsburgh National Bank	8/12/81	19.00	20.71	10,019,821
5,000,000	Republic National Bank, Dallas	8/20/81	18.63	20.27	5,009,420
10,000,000	Security Pacific National Bank	7/15/81	15.42	16.60	9,994,510
10,000,000	Security Pacific National Bank	7/21/81	15.20	16.33	9,996,396
5,000,000	Security Pacific National Bank	7/23/81	15.70	16.92	4,990,981
5,000,000	Security Pacific National Bank	10/26/81	18.00	19.23	4,972,566
4,000,000	United California Bank	7/6/81	15.20	16.01	4,000,348
$264,500,000	Total certificates of deposit			18.27%	$264,327,887

Face amount (B)		Due date	Interest rates at date of purchase: Stated rate	Interest rates at date of purchase: Annualized yield (C)	Market value (D)
COMMERCIAL PAPER (36.2%)					
$5,000,000	Abbott Laboratories	7/7/81	17.13%	19.17%	$ 4,902,953
7,000,000	Abbott Laboratories	7/8/81	17.38	19.41	6,903,075
6,000,000	Abbott Laboratories	7/16/81	17.13	19.14	5,901,536
10,000,000	Abbott Laboratories	7/17/81	16.63	18.50	9,857,091
5,000,000	Abbott Laboratories	7/28/81	16.75	18.68	4,919,472
8,000,000	Crown Zellerbach Corp	7/1/81	17.20	19.22	7,870,044
10,000,000	Crown Zellerbach Corp	7/17/81	17.00	18.99	9,827,314
9,500,000	Crown Zellerbach Corp	7/31/81	17.00	18.98	9,346,949
10,000,000	Deere & Co	7/14/81	17.25	19.28	9,844,343
10,000,000	Dow Chemical Co	7/15/81	17.25	19.28	9,844,546
10,000,000	Dow Chemical Co	7/22/81	17.00	18.98	9,837,454
9,300,000	Dow Chemical Co	7/30/81	17.00	18.98	9,150,015
5,000,000	Dow Chemical Co	7/31/81	16.75	18.69	4,912,688
10,000,000	Getty Oil Co	7/17/81	17.00	18.96	9,860,244
11,000,000	Halliburton Corp	7/6/81	17.20	19.25	10,795,994
12,000,000	Halliburton Corp	7/9/81	16.00	17.78	11,795,784
10,000,000	Halliburton Corp	7/14/81	17.75	19.91	9,826,838
13,000,000	Mobil Oil Credit Corp	7/13/81	17.13	19.12	12,804,492
10,000,000	Mobil Oil Credit Corp	7/27/81	16.75	18.66	9.852,726
15,000,000	Phillips Petroleum Credit Corp	7/10/81	17.00	18.96	14,789,016
10,000,000	Phillips Petroleum Credit Corp	7/13/81	17.25	19.27	9,853,697

6,000,000	Phillips Petroleum Credit Corp	7/16/81	17.25	19.26	5,915,445
11,000,000	Schering-Plough Corp	7/1/81	17.00	18.91	10,890,917
5,000,000	Schering-Plough Corp	7/7/81	19.00	21.36	4,954,464
5,000,000	Southwestern Bell Telephone Co.	7/10/81	16.50	18.39	4,910,542
7,000,000	Standard Oil of Indiana	7/6/81	17.13	19.09	6,913,909
5,000,000	Superior Oil Co	7/2/81	17.13	19.14	4,916,826
6,000,000	Texas Oil & Gas Corp	7/16/81	17.25	19.21	5,944,092
12,000,000	Union Oil Credit Corp	7/8/81	17.50	19.56	11,832,929
7,000,000	Union Oil Credit Corp	7/14/81	16.75	18.65	6,905,961
$259,800,000	**Total commercial paper**			**19.10%**	**$255,881,356**
U.S. GOVERNMENT OBLIGATIONS (18.2%)					
$ 10,000,000	Federal Farm Credit Bank DN	7/6/81	16.75%	18.60%	$ 9,908,462
20,000,000	Federal Farm Credit Bank DN	7/6/81	18.00	20.10	19,866,458
13,000,000	Federal Farm Credit Bank DN	7/6/81	18.00	20.10	12,913,198
22,000,000	Federal Farm Credit Bank DN	7/7/81	15.75	17.35	21,923,176
23,000,000	Federal Farm Credit Bank DN	7/13/81	15.75	17.37	22,859,808
5,000,000	Federal Home Loan Bank DN	7/30/81	14.25	16.04	4,721,887
5,000,000	Federal Home Loan Bank DN	8/4/81	14.00	15.74	4,716,963
5,000,000	Federal Home Loan Bank DN	8/6/81	12.20	13.51	4,758,256
5,000,000	Federal Home Loan Bank DN	8/7/81	12.20	13.51	4,756,461
6,000,000	Federal Home Loan Bank DN	10/9/81	13.00	14.69	5,549,104
8,000,000	Federal Home Loan Bank DN	12/1/81	15.40	17.68	7,422,743
5,000,000	Federal Home Loan Bank DN	12/2/81	15.00	17.16	4,641,292
5,000,000	Federal Home Loan Bank DN	12/28/81	14.65	16.81	4,599,467
$132,000,000	**Total U.S. Government Obligations**			**17.61%**	**$128,637,275**

Face amount (B)		Due date	Interest rates at date of purchase — Stated rate	Interest rates at date of purchase — Annualized yield (C)	Market value (D)
BANK REPURCHASE AGREEMENTS (6.9%)					
$ 48,968,000	Continental Illinois Bank & Trust Co. (Collateralized by $58,755,000 Federal Home Loan Bank Notes, 10.45% due 2/25/87)............................	7/1/78	14.88%	16.27%	$ 48,968,000
$ 48,968,000	**Total bank repurchase agreements**			16.27%	$ 48,968,000
	Cash and receivables, net of liabilities (1.3%)				$ 9,372,544
Net assets (100%) (Equivalent to $1.00 per share)					$707,187,062

NOTES:

(A) Annualized yield to investors represents current day's dividend annualized on a daily compound basis. Net income fluctuates each day and may be subject to significant changes depending upon the future level of interest rates.

(B) Represents the principal amount of the obligation, not its cost to DIF.

(C) Annualized yield for each security assumes consistent reinvestment of its principal and interest or discount at the existing rate and maturity term.

(D) Market value is equal to maturity value discounted at current interest rates for remaining days to maturity and excluding accrued interest receivable.

A share in the Fund for the calendar month (30 days) earned .01367. This converts to a 17.96% annual yield on a daily compound basis.

NOTE: Reprinted by permission of Reich & Tang.

When I analyzed the quality of the holdings in this fund compared with those in some of the other funds that had sent me portfolios in answer to my request for up-to-date information, I realized that Daily Income Fund is managed by a team of pros who know their business and stick faithfully to the fund's objective: "to provide high current income to the extent consistent with the preservation of capital."

Incidentally, a year prior to the exhibited holdings of Daily Income, the fund had assets of about $536 million. On June 31, 1981, Daily Income's assets were $707 million. The fund grew by 32% in that one year—without advertising itself the way some other funds I've mentioned earlier have been doing. A question worth pondering is what the actual net yield will be to shareholders of money funds that are aggressively advertising, after deduction of media expenses in 1981.

Let me make it clear, though, that I am not necessarily making a recommendation for you to send money to Daily Income—or to any other money fund, for that matter. I *know* what I want to do with my money. And I hope you, as a smart investor, will get to know what to do with yours.

Miscellaneous Considerations

In addition to examining any money fund portfolio and rating it either with my yardsticks for safety and yield or with anyone else's, including your own, you should give some weight to who is promoting (distributing) the fund and who the paid investment advisers are. All this can be found in the prospectus; and you can readily receive a copy from any fund offered to the public that's blue skyed in your state.

Somewhere in the course of my research on money market investments, I began to develop the conviction that institutional money market funds are managed a bit more conservatively—at least from the safety standpoint—than are general purpose funds. To prove my point, just glance at the "institutions only" funds displayed in the table from Donoghue's *Money Fund Report*. Notice that *only* Dreyfus Money Market contains any Euro-paper in its portfolio. All the others have none. But this is certainly not the case with general purpose or stockbroker/general purpose funds. Just see for yourself how many of these funds contain offshore paper.

The final factor in attempting to evaluate whether or not a particular fund is for you is, of course, the *bottom line*. What will you actually *receive* in the form of monthly payout from the fund's daily compounding? Notice underneath the listing of the Daily Income portfolio that there is a box that reads, in part: "A share in the Fund for the calendar month (30 days) earned .01367." This means that a $1,000 investment earned $13.67 for the period compounded daily, or annualized at 17.96% *if the portfolio were to earn that kind of gross every month for a year*! If I intended to invest in Daily Income, or any other fund, I'd want to see what has been earned and what has been paid out to shareholders on a monthly basis, at least for the past six months. That is why there have been a string of lawsuits against many money funds, including Daily Income and my wife's fund out West, seeking a reduction in charges against income by the management and the distributors.

Now that you have peeked into a money fund portfolio and have been given some basic guidelines to help you understand better what you may be buying or already have risked in money fund investments, it is time to revisit the funds and look at their differences.

7
Money Funds Revisited

Donoghue's *Money Fund Report* for July 13, 1981, lists 66 general purpose funds, sponsored by investment company (mutual fund) managements; 34 stockbroker/general purpose funds, distributed by New York Stock Exchange firms; and 16 institutions-only funds, distributed in some instances by mutual fund managements and in others by stockbrokers.* Shares in both general purpose categories are available to the investing public. There are some very sound business reasons for investment company managements and stockbrokers to involve themselves with the offering of no-load money funds, so let's take a closer look at them.

Investment Company Funds

The primary business of investment company managements is to attract new money to add to existing or newly formed mutual funds that either bear a front-end load charge or are no-load with hidden charges. The ICI lists the load-bearing mutual funds by investment categories:

* A listing of funds that are members of the Investment Company Institute is to be found in Appendix A. Certain stockbroker-sponsored money funds like Hutton's Cash Reserve are not ICI members.

Aggressive Growth
Balanced
Bond
Growth
Growth and Income
Income
Limited Maturity Municipal
Municipal Bond
Options

The front-end load for small investments of $1,000 to $10,000 runs from 6% to 8% of the investment. The investment company managements sponsoring these load funds usually retain 2% of the load, passing the rest on to brokers or salesmen who vend the fund shares to the public. When money funds began to be popular some years ago, many investors liquidated mutual fund shares to invest in the kind of no-load shares that were restricted only to money market investments.

That is why investment company managements began to jump into the money fund money pool—with very little to gain from the investment of other people's money in the money market since there were no front-end loads on most of the funds and since the investment advisory fees are basically much smaller than in the case of load-bearing mutual funds.

But the leap into money funds by investment company managements was not merely defensive: it meant that if investors wanted to get into money funds they could simply switch from the growth fund they were carrying into the money fund distributed by the same management. Moreover, a mass of dollars invested in a money fund under the management of an investment company offering other types of load-bearing funds would, of course, be available for switching if conditions in the interest rate markets worsened and yields of the money funds dropped.

For example, Putnam manages 12 mutual funds, including its no-load money fund. By advertising continually for new investors to its money fund, Putnam will have a future pool of money in its no-load fund that investors may someday switch to a load fund—if investment conditions warrant such a switch—and save themselves anywhere from 2% to 8%, depending on how large the amount of funds switched actually is.

Insurance companies that have entered the money fund management field also have good reasons for their efforts. Some of them seek to gather a concentrated pool of investor funds so that they can offer those investors similar no-cost switching to other load funds sponsored by the insurance companies. John Hancock, for example, offers six mutual funds, two of which are money funds. Mutual of Omaha offers five funds, one of which is a no-load money fund. The Kemper organization offers nine funds, of which one is a no-load money market fund. And so it goes.

Understandably, insurance companies have another motive for sponsoring no-load money market funds—the money fund shareholders are potential purchasers of some kind of insurance policy from the sponsoring management.

Stockbroker-Sponsored Funds

Competing intensely for investors' dollars, large stockbrokerage firms have become securely entrenched as leaders in marketing money fund shares of funds allied with or sponsored by the firms themselves. And with good reason.

"In the beginning," admitted E. F. Hutton's Thomas Lynch, "we used Dreyfus Liquid Assets. But we soon saw the sense in doing our own thing and we got into Cash Reserve Management." You cannot invest directly in this fund by sending it money. You have to visit a Hutton office, or have a Hutton broker visit you and open an account at Hutton.

To open an account registered with Cash Reserve Management, but maintained as an account at Hutton, requires a minimum of $10,000. The dividends you will earn at Cash Reserve Management are credited directly to your account at Hutton, and the statement of transactions in your fund account will come not from the fund but from Hutton.

One of the advantages of dealing directly with a stockbroker to purchase shares of the fund that firm sponsors is simply convenience. Hutton, Merrill Lynch, Dean Witter, Thomson McKinnon, and other giant brokerage firms maintain branches all over the globe so that you can deposit funds into your account in London or San Francisco or New York and the shares you purchase will be earning money market dividends the same or the next day, depending upon when the brokerage firm's computer "sees" your money. I estimate the difference between dropping off a check at a broker's office for fund purchase and mailing money to a money fund sponsored by an investment company is about nine days in terms of money market dividends.

Another advantage of having a broker-connected money fund account is ready withdrawal. You can phone your broker in the morning and chances are a check will be ready for you to pick up after lunch. It will be a broker's check that you can, if need be, certify the same day, rather than a check from a money fund whose headquarters are located in Cincinnati or in San Mateo, California.

But if stockbroker-related money funds are a convenience for you, they are also a marketing tool for the brokerage firm services. Merrill Lynch, for example, offers a cash management account that permits any investor to control money in five rather interesting ways.

1. Your idle money is invested in Merrill's money fund to be compounded daily as dividends at high money market rates.
2. You can have instant access to your money simply by writing a check ($500 or more).
3. You have instant access to a credit line based on your securities value.
4. You receive a special Visa charge card that has a special credit line.
5. You get a single monthly statement summarizing securities transactions, dividend and check activities, and Visa card activities.

To get started in Merrill Lynch's cash management program takes at least $20,000, but not all of it will go into the money fund Merrill sponsors. Some of it is left for investment or speculation, depending on what you want. In its "total" cash management approach, Merrill Lynch therefore not only provides money fund access but it also serves your credit and securities needs.

Jerry Rosen, Group W Broadcasting's personal finance correspondent, advised his listeners one morning on the radio to split their money equally between several funds—some broker sponsored and some sponsored by investment company managements. While his reasoning involved safety of principal, it turns out that this is a very practical money-making suggestion because of the ability to invest almost instantly through a broker, and because it takes a long time for a money fund check to clear in New York or Boston if it's drawn on a bank in Houston, Texas, or Palo Alto, California. You will see an example of this in my next chapter, on personal money fund strategies.

Specialty Money Funds

Marketing of money fund shares has become a highly competitive affair between the investment company and the brokerage sponsors, so that there have developed during 1981 several groups of specialty funds. These funds, like all other money funds, operate in the money market, but they have specialized their portfolios so that the major segment of their investment risk is confined to one special section of the money market.

Thus we have a growing number of funds that are being marketed because of the "safety," since they consist mainly of government and agency obligations. Tax-free money funds (that is, free only from federal taxation) are also increasing. (These will be discussed in detail in Chapter 10, dealing with money fund taxation.)

So far only Value Line Cash Fund and Oppenheimer Monetary Bridge seem to have decided to specialize in commercial paper. It is not too farfetched to envision some funds specializing only in CDs at some future date. Future specialization, I guess, will depend on where yield and safety rank among investor requirements.

8
Personal Money Fund Strategies

It would be difficult to find a money-management tool during the first seven months of 1981 that would have multiplied anybody's money better than investments in money funds. The proof of this rests in the following graph:

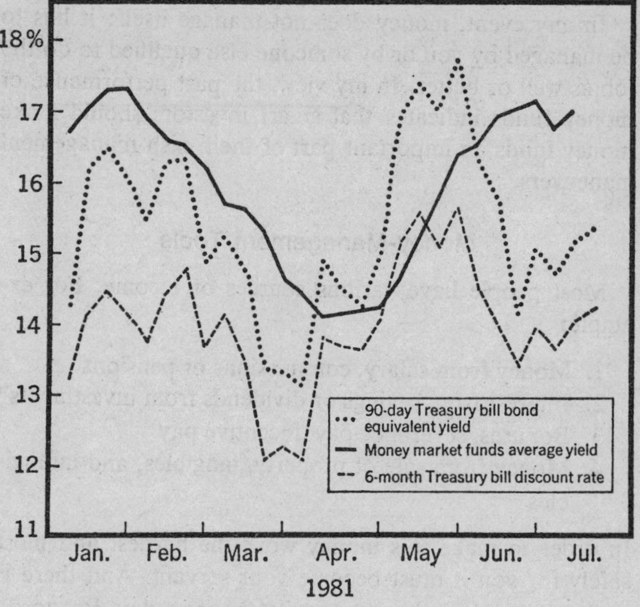

Note: Reprinted courtesy of the Bank of New York.

Note that except for very brief intervals the average money fund dividend yield exceeded both the 90-day and the 6-month T-bill yields. But what the chart doesn't show is how our money grows by daily compounding in the money fund. Thus, if you had invested an equal sum, say $10,000, in a money fund and the discounted value of the 6-month bills, which of course would be less than $10,000, in February, and liquidated the fund shares at the time the 6-month bills matured, you would have earned more than the indicated rate on the money fund investment.

Naturally, there is no guarantee that money fund yields will not slip dramatically if rates go down drastically during the next six months—but so will the T-bill rates go down.

In any event, money does not manage itself: it has to be managed by you or by someone else qualified to do the job as well or better. In my view, the past performance of money funds indicates that smart investors should make money funds an important part of their cash management maneuvers.

Money-Management Tools

Most people have various sources of income. For example:

1. Money from salary, commissions or pensions
2. Interest from savings or dividends from investments
3. Bonuses, severance pay, incentive pay
4. Money from sale of property, tangibles, and intangibles

In order to make this money work the hardest and most safely for you it must become your servant. And there is no law against working money 24 hours a day. But to do this properly as a smart investor you have to have proper money-management tools. If your approach to money multiplication *doesn't involve risk*, the number of money-management tools needed decreases in number. Here's what you need if you want to eliminate almost all of the risk in managing your money:

1. An insured bank or thrift account sufficiently large to cash either your paycheck or a money fund check (most money fund checks are a minimum of $500)
2. An account at any money fund listed in Appendix A that is rated at least R or better for safety and PG for yield

What you do after opening a money fund account for the amount you have available—the minimum is usually $1,000—is to deposit your paycheck from then on (if it's over $100, the minimum at most funds) by mailing it to the fund. The next day you can go to your bank or thrift and cash a money fund check for the amount of your paycheck or less (but it must be at least $500). By doing this you'll earn money fund dividends on your paycheck from the time it reaches your fund, and your account won't be debited for the amount of the money fund check until it clears. But you must make sure that you are dealing with funds like Putnam Daily Dividend or Fidelity Cash, who have arrangements with their clearing bank to convert checks received into fund shares for your account the day after the fund receives your check.

Innovative investors will readily understand that you can only take advantage of these extra earnings twice a month because most banks and thrifts won't turn an out-of-town check, like your money fund one on a bank based in Boston or Denver, into "good funds" for 14 days. Thus, assuming you had $2,000 in one of the accommodating money funds and a $2,000 balance in a bank or thrift, how much money could you utilize in this "float" maneuver twice a month? Since most funds require that you leave a balance of over $500, I would suggest using $1,000 to float between your bank and your money fund. Assuming that your paycheck was $1,000 net and you cashed a money fund check at the bank or thrift for $1,-000, and it took the check you cashed from the money fund 8 days to clear, triggering a sale of $1,000 worth of money fund shares from your account, and 6 days of float on your $1,000 paycheck, how much extra would you have earned? If the fund paid 16%, or 44¢ a day on $1,-000, you'd be making 88¢ a day on the $2,000 increase in your fund account for 6 days, and 44¢ a day on $1,000 for the 2 extra days of float on the check you cashed at the bank or thrift. This would amount to $6.16. If you did this with $10,000, the earnings would be $61.60, less the cost of the stationery and the stamp to send your paycheck or any other check to the money fund.

An improvement on this float strategy is to have an account at a broker connected with a stockbroker/general purpose fund and also an account at a fund like Putnam, Fidelity, or any other money fund that will convert your check into shares the day after receipt. This obviously requires somewhat more investment capital. If you have an account at a broker, your paycheck can be deposited before lunch on payday into your brokerage account and shares in the broker-related fund will be purchased for your fund account that very day. That afternoon you send a check for a similar amount to the money fund sponsored by the investment company in Boston, Denver, or wherever to buy shares in that fund. In the meantime, you go into your bank where you have "good money" on deposit and cash a money fund check drawn not on the broker-related fund but on the fund in Boston or Denver, which will take eight days to clear.

You can earn even more on your float between the *two* funds and the float at the bank where you cashed the out-of-town money check. Assume your paycheck was

$2,000 and your money fund checks (one drawn on the broker-related fund, one drawn on the accommodating investment-company-managed fund) were a total of $2,000 ($1,000 each). Don't forget, this time your paycheck earned a full eight-day float from the broker-related fund and six days from the non-broker-related fund. In the meantime, the check you handed the bank from the non-broker-related fund also earned eight days; and the check from the broker-related fund to the non-broker-related fund to buy shares in the latter fund earned six days' float.

If you really want to get the *most* out of your money you need two broker-related funds and two non-broker-related general purpose funds. Grab a pencil and figure out how much extra you could earn on $2,000 or $10,000 by moving the money around in a managed fashion between the broker funds and the non-broker funds—*without cashing anything at a bank.* If you do cash money fund checks at a bank while doing this floating, you have to be aware of how long the bank will take to clear each check. But if you don't cash any money fund checks during these maneuvers, you can float away to almost undreamed-of daily yields if the money funds average 17% or higher. And suppose money fund yields dropped to 14%? You'd still be able to earn more with an efficient floating schedule and system than you can with any other low-risk medium.

Payment Delay Means Extra Money

Another money management tool you can use is simply to *delay payment as long as possible*. It seems that a lot of companies are doing this. You read about corporations increasing their cash flow simply by holding back payment of bills for anything from magazine subcriptions to drinking water for the office. Of course, they do pay eventually, but they earn plenty on the cash generated from not issuing checks before the bills are actually due and payable.

In my opinion, the best personal means of delaying payment of any cash purchases is the *credit card*. Normally I charge everything I can to credit cards and then *pay the monthly bills in full on the due date with a money fund check*. I charge my gasoline, my meats, my dining out, my travel expenses—indeed *everything* possible that can be charged to one or the other of my credit cards—and *pay the bills with a money fund check before incurring any finance charges*. (Of course, if you want to be able to pay with a money fund check, your credit card bill must be at least $500 each month. I don't find this to be a problem at all.)

Do make sure, however, that you pay the credit card bills on the date they are due so as not to incur any finance charges. At current 22% per year on the unpaid balance in charge card accounts, it doesn't make sense to incur loan charges by making small monthly payments—unless you can figure out how to earn at a higher rate than the charges levied for the money left unpaid at the end of each month.

The use of credit cards to delay payment can become quite significant if you travel to Europe or the Far East, as I do almost every year. Actually, I discovered the millenium in the spring of 1981 when I made a trip to Hong Kong and Australia. Over the course of 25 years I have cemented a very fine credit relationship with a certain travel agency in Philadelphia. My practice with this agency is to have them ticket my trip—and I pay them upon my return. It would be almost criminal to reveal what the cost was for round-trip tickets from New York to Hong Kong and thence to Brisbane, Melbourne, and Sydney, Australia, and back home via Los Angeles. I could have bought a Pan Am world airpass for $1,750 if my trip would have consumed at least 22 days. But I could only remain away for 17 days and thus had to pay far more.

Of course, a person of my corporate stature stays only at the best hotels, including the Mandarin in Hong Kong, possibly one of the most luxurious hotels in the world. But I made the whole trip with credit cards and credit at the travel agency.

It took the Mandarin Hotel's charges better than two months to appear on my credit card statement—and I paid that on the due date, a month later. It took slightly less than two months for the charges at the Reef House in Cairns and the bills from the Hiltons in Melbourne and Sydney to hit my credit card account, and money fund checks were relayed in payment on the credit card statement due date. The travel agency got the fare via a money fund check on my return.

No sooner did I get back to my office than I was reimbursed for the portion of my trip attributable to my firm. The day I received this check it went over to my broker-related money fund and was converted into money fund shares that multiplied daily for me while I awaited the arrival of the credit card charges. By *smart money management through delayed payment I managed to make extra money fund dividends on my credit* not only while travelling but after I returned from the trip.

But looking back now I realize I could have been even smarter. How? I could have gotten an advance from my firm for the trip's expenses and deposited that in the money fund to earn high money fund dividends while I was swimming in the Coral Sea.

In times of high interest rates it's important to make as much as you can from delayed payment. For example, real estate taxes are normally due and payable twice a year where I live. The July 1 payment is actually due on August 10. But naturally the bill for the taxes arrives on June 1. In my house, that bill gets stuffed in a pigeonhole inside my desk and is hauled out and mailed on August 10—with a money fund check that won't clear until perhaps August 20.

So imagine my amazement on the first Saturday in June when I saw a financial idiot withdraw the thousands of dollars for county taxes due August 10 from his passbook account and convert the money into a bank money order. Thereupon he carefully inserted the bank check with the proper tax stub and mailed the envelope to the county treasurer.

What crime against himself had this man committed? By withdrawing from his savings account, where he earns 5½% from day of deposit to day of withdrawal, he lost the earning power on the withdrawn funds for at *least two months*!

Another area of delayed payment involves the estimated tax that people who earn over $25,000 a year normally file during four quarters of a calendar year. This estimated quarterly advance tax payment on money the taxpayer might not earn is burdensome at any interest rate levels. But when money funds throw off over 17% and the penalty for underpayment is only 12%, growing numbers of taxpayers keep reserve money in their money fund accounts and make a lump-sum payment on January 15, preceding the April 15 filing date. Thus for at least three-quarters of the year they are earning high money market yields instead of withdrawing the money quarterly and passing it on to the government.

In summary, I am confident that if you use your innovative talents you'll come up with many ways to generate money from delayed payment—without having bill collectors hound you or levy law suits.

You never have to pay for *any* legal debt under the laws of the United States until that debt is due and payable. Don't be snowed under by schools, charities, magazines, or anyone else who sends you bills months in advance. If charity begins at home, as the saying goes, send a money fund check when your money has to leave home—not before.

Raising Extra Cash for Money Fund Investment

This leads me to the next personal money management ploy: raising extra cash for investment. When interest rates are high, it is difficult to generate cash via loans on real property, securities, or other holdings. Mortgage rates are at about the same level as the return on money fund investments; call loans to brokers exceed 19%, and investors with stocks they can borrow on would have to pay 20% and perhaps more. So the normal strategy of raising money by borrowing on tangibles or intangibles is temporarily out. Of course, if conditions in the interest rate markets are such that loans on property or securities are offered for less than the yield on low-risk investments like money funds, it might make sense to hock your house or your AT&T shares. Then, when the return from the funds dips below the cost of the loans, liquidate the fund shares and pay off the loans.

But there are many other areas where investors may be able to generate cash to take advantage of currently high money market rates earned by the money funds. These include:

1. *Investments*, tangible and intangible, that are held at a loss or are not earning a high enough yield to warrant continuing to hold them
2. *Advances*, from employers or friends, non–interest bearing
3. *Loans from relatives*, non–interest bearing, of course, if possible, or low interest if not
4. *Prepayment*, for goods or services

Let's look at each of these categories.

If you hold securities or mutual fund shares that have little chance of rebounding so you can dispose of them without a loss, it makes sense to dispose of them to establish tax losses that reduce income and provide cash that can multiply in a money fund or other high-paying interest account, insured or uninsured. In some instances, the tangibles sold at a loss could be substituted in another form, thus freeing up cash and still allowing you to retain an investment in the area to take advantage of a possible rebound. For example, if you own 100 ounces of gold that you paid $800 an ounce for in January 1980, and gold is down to $400 an ounce in August 1981, you are sitting with a $40,000 loss. In 1978 gold advanced 37%; in 1979 it advanced almost 100%; but in 1981 it dropped over 50% from its 1980 high. By selling the gold at a loss and simultaneously substituting one contract of gold futures on a commodity exchange you would free up $38,000 ($2,000 is for margin) of cash that could be placed in your broker's money fund to earn money while waiting for gold to come back—if it ever does.

But in the meantime the $40,000 you had locked up in the physical gold has been converted to futures, releasing most of the cash locked up in the loss, earning you a fine yield on the principal, and providing you with a tax loss that can reduce your income tax liability to boot.

You may have real property that is not earning enough through rental or is vacant and actually losing you money. At 18% your money doubles in four years if compounded. Doesn't it make sense to dispose of unprofitable real estate and earn big money on the released funds?

A smart investor seeks to cull losers from his possessions and use that money formerly locked up to earn as much more money as possible. You might think to yourself at this point, why only dispose of losers? Why not winners? And the answer, traditionally, is that with investments you cut losses quickly and let winners run.

But that's if you are involved in real risk. In the world of money funds the risk has been considerably minimized, and the prime considerations are safety and yield when choosing funds for investment, not the possibility of capital gains or losses.

The second sensible area of raising extra cash to work for you in the money market is through advances. Key bank employees, for example, can obtain interest-free loans from their banks. What better purpose of any loan than to generate more income for the borrower than the cost of carrying the loan? It would be a safe guess to speculate that if bank employees are able to get such long-term loans from their banks, part of the funds will wind up in money fund accounts.

I have already pointed out the advantage of obtaining a substantial advance from your firm if you have to go on business trips. Put the check you receive as an advance in a money fund and pay the credit card bills one month or more after the trip is over, earning dividends both on the advance and on the delayed bill payment via the charge-card money-fund payment route.

There is a fantasy I have had for some years as I have approached retirement. I know at least 2,000 people I can approach and borrow $100 from—without any interest and without any specific time table for repayment. Since many of these friends have at one time or other approached me for the same favor, I figure it would take me about two weeks to gather up $200,000 in this manner. Then I would open four money fund accounts (two at brokers) for $50,000 each and spend my retirement floating away while moving my fund money around. Of course, to make sure these fine friends were properly repaid I'd leave them $100 each in my will.

My son scoffed at this grandiose but perfectly legal

scheme to raise investment money from friends, and said, "Why go to all that trouble? If rates remained at 17%, what would you have left out of the $34,000 a year after taxes?" Then he suggested, "Why not go to the bank and buy $200,000 face value of E Bonds, issuing each $100 bond in each lender's name and mailing it on maturity. That way you won't have to be bothered with a lengthy will—and besides, you'd generate for yourself $50,000 *tax-free.*"

Stunned at this suggestion, I asked him to explain.

"You only have to lay out $150,000 to buy $200,000 face value of $100 bonds. So you'd immediately generate $50,000 in extra cash. Since the whole $200,000 is a loan you have no tax liability on the $50,000."

Silently I wondered if the recipients of the $100 face value bonds would have to pay taxes on the appreciation when they cashed their bonds in. But then I mused, "Who ever paid all their taxes on "E" bonds—and besides, they're gifts."

Naturally I will never get around to fulfilling my financial fantasy, but I mention it to spur you to be creative in thinking about raising extra cash from friends, who might already have borrowed from you.

Relatives are, of course, another source you can approach for interest-free loans, or for loans bearing interest lower than the money fund payouts. If you have to return the money, you can liquidate the fund shares and return the money; the compounded dividends, of course, will be yours.

The final broad category of ways to raise cash quickly involves prepayment for either goods or services. You may be in a small business and have inventory that someone wants to buy eventually but cannot store. Get an advance or prepayment on the goods and earn money market interest via money fund dividends. If you are an author, you'll normally receive a significant advance to write a book. Put the advance where it can work hardest for you, because it will take at least a year and a half after you finish the manuscript before you'll get a royalty statement.

Of course, you can also raise cash via garage sales, selling off antiques or just plain junk that lie moldering in your attic or basement. The point is that there are all sorts of ways for you to winnow out losers, raise extra cash wherever you can—and make your money work hardest for you while interest rates remain high.

Some Switching Strategies

You may have read, or heard, that it makes sense to invest in more than one money fund—and then switch to whichever funds are earning more than the ones you are in.

In the first place, from my own personal experience, you should invest in a money fund where making deposits is quite convenient. I do not rely too much upon the mails any more, and I maintain a brokerage-related money fund account. Thus I can make instant deposits near where I work, without expense or delay of postal operation; and I can make ready withdrawals by calling my broker for a check, which he can cash for me after I endorse it.

Admittedly I maintain a rather large pool of reserve funds with my broker because I'm pleased with the performance of the money fund and the convenience of always being able to deposit "good money" (no matter where the deposited check comes from) and withdraw good money from the brokerage account. Moreover, I am adequately supplied with checks and updated information—without the expense of writing elsewhere to get this from a non-broker-related money fund. That is why, if my fund pays 17% for 30 days and I notice an ad from a competing money fund that announces 17.58% for a 7-day period, I do not switch. But if my fund were to drop a whole percentage point below the average yield of the general purpose money funds, I certainly would think of making a switch, provided the fund I intended to switch into measured up to my rather conservative safety standards.

If you have $4,000 invested in one money fund that you find performs well, and whose safety level you are satisfied with, does it make sense to switch some of the money into, say, three other funds so that your $4,000 will be diversified into four fund accounts of $1,000 each?

Frankly, I don't think so. This means you would have to open at least four envelopes a month, check four money fund statements a month, and if you are writing any checks on these funds the total number of checks you could write and still maintain minimum balances in these funds would be *four* at $500 each, leaving $500 balances in each of the funds. If, on the other hand, you had $4,000 invested in a money fund that offered check-writing privileges, you could write *seven* $500 checks and still maintain the minimum balance in your lone fund account.

Some people regard money fund accounts as pools that can be added to at regular intervals. Assuming you had $200 extra to park in a money fund—and most funds require minimum additional investments to be at least $100—you could only buy more shares in two funds, using two envelopes, stamps, and so forth. If you maintained four money funds you'd have to decide which two you wanted to add to with the $200. Now, what if the week after your investment addition had been mailed away for purchase, the two neglected funds reported better yields than the two selected for further investment?

I frankly don't know how much sense there is in carrying four, six, or eight accounts at money funds. But evidently many people think that's the thing to do, because the more than 8 million current money fund accounts certainly *do not* represent 8 million different people. (The best estimate is probably 1 million-plus people.)

When should you switch then; if your fund's earnings continue to be near the industry average? I would say when the fund alters its investment approach radically by shifting to riskier investments in the money market than those it held when you became a shareholder. For example, if you invested in a fund that confined purchases of CDs to banks with above $100,000,000 in assets, you might think of changing when that fund sent you an update announcing future purchase of CDs also from banks under $100-million.

Money Fund Allocation

Finally, there are the personal decisions you have to make about how much you want to park in which money fund, or funds, and how often you want to add to those accounts.

As part of any smart investor's approach to return on investment, certain portions of available and reserve monies may be used for a variety of purposes, including safekeeping, low-risk investments, and risk investments. At the start of this book I attempted to explain that money fund investments are not safe investments but may be considered "practically safe" because they deal in very short-term investments that are regarded mainly as "safe" and you can withdraw your investment at any time without cost or penalty. Does that mean you should put all, or most, of your liquid assets into money funds?

Definitely not. Don't go overboard. Keep a sensible part of your "rainy day" or emergency cash in a bank or thrift that's convenient for you to make deposits and withdrawals without the expense of travelling to it. While it is true that there has been a geometric rise in money fund purchases by former depositors in banks and thrifts, money funds still do not extend credit. And a personal or home loan might be needed for some unforeseen emergency, such as when you have to repair a leaky roof and the expense is more than you have available in your money fund account.

Some money fund advocates have begun to consider people who still keep money in a savings account "misfits." But that's baloney. Just try to open a charge account at a department store or apply for a credit card and leave blank spaces on the application forms that ask you for information about your checking and savings accounts.

You have to *manage* your money so that the reserve funds and additions to any money fund accounts fit within the framework of your own personal income/expense situation. But if you do plunge too heavily into money funds during times of exceedingly high short-term interest rates, at least you can be sure that it's possible to withdraw the funds quickly by check, wire, or telephone when you need them.

So if you become overenthusiastic in using money funds as money management tools you can always draw a check to curb your exuberance. After all, rates are not going to stay at the present high levels forever.

9

Money Market Fun—and Games

If you are reluctant to have money fund managers invest your money in the exciting money market, but would rather play that game yourself for fun and profit, you need several key ingredients.

1. Plenty of cash and/or credit
2. Close contact with specialists at money market banks and brokers
3. A continuous flow of timely statistical and technical information on both interest rates and the availability of money market debt instruments
4. The ability to forecast rather accurately interest-rate direction in the near-term and long-term
5. The good fortune to consistently make the kind of money market debt investment selections that will result in gains, not losses

Obviously, these are exacting and formidable requirements for a successful money-market venture of your own. Perhaps that is why so many institutional and commercial investors as well as private investors leave the selection, supervision, and management, including the timing of market entry and exit of the involved securities, to the money market pros who manage the money funds.

But if you do have the finances and/or the credit connections and want to play this sophisticated game for personal profits, you certainly should try it.

The main money market game is *profiting from changes in the interest rates.* The basic principle that gains you money in this game is simple: "Up is down; down is up." If interest rates go up, the cost to buyers of existing money market instruments traded in the secondary (resale) market goes down. If interest rates decline, the cost to buyers rises. And the main arena, where more than $3 billion worth of these instruments trade each day, is the U.S. Government bond and note securities markets.

The No-Loss Game

Since investors who play this market presumably are less concerned with interest income, which is taxable (except for federal taxation on T-bill yields), than they are with long- and short-term capital gains, chances are their principal activity will be with long-term bonds and notes, rather than with short-term T-bills. Moreover, there isn't very much of a secondary securities market in such money market instruments as commercial paper, CDs, and BAs, so for purposes of illustrating how an investor can make money in this trading game, we will stick to government bonds and notes that have been issued long ago and are currently available in the secondary government securities markets.

I have already mentioned that the N.Y. Fed issues a daily listing of representative secondary government bond and note offerings that are published in the financial sections of leading newspapers. And publications like *The New York Times, Wall Street Journal,* and *Barron's* devote a good deal of space in almost every issue to money market conditions and interest rates, besides listing government note and bond offerings.

The way you make gains in this game is to *resell what*

you buy for a profit, and *earn interest* while waiting to sell.

But might you not also be moved to sell at a loss if you misjudged interest-rate direction? Of course, you could lose money if you sold. But in this game if you have sufficient finances there *never is any reason to lose money.* Because whatever you buy—government notes or bonds at below par ($1,000, expressed as "100")—will bring you the *full* amount of the instrument upon maturity.

By way of illustration, look at this note offered on August 18, 1981:

Issue	*Bid*	*Ask*	*Yield*
Nov. '82-n-7⅛%	90.10	90.14	15.90

It runs for more than a year from August 18 so if you bought and held it to maturity you'd earn $71.25 interest per annum on each $1,000 face value in the note—plus a long-term capital gain on the difference between your cost of the note (90.14, which is $900 + 14/32, or 14 × 31.25¢, for a total bond cost of $904.38) and the par (100 = $1,000) maturity value when it is redeemed. Calculating the interest return on a 365-day year for the 433-day holding period of this investment, here are the results on a $100,000 trade:

Interest on $100,000, 7.125% notes for 433 days	$8,452.16
Long-term capital gain between cost of $90,438 and face value of $100,000	$9,562.00
Total interest and capital gain to maturity, November 1, 1981, from August 18, 1981, purchase date	$18,014.16

Since only $90,438 was used to generate this combination of interest and long-term gain, the return on investment is calculated:

$$\text{Investment return} = \frac{\$18{,}014.16 \text{ earnings}}{\$90{,}438} = 19.92\%$$

Of course, this was earned over a 433-day holding period so the return for one year would be:

$$\frac{\$18{,}014.16}{433 \text{ days}} = \$41.60/\text{day}$$

$$\$41.60/\text{day} \times 365 \text{ days} = 15.184\%$$

The yield listed in the newspaper of 15.90 comes from a yield to maturity formula that expresses as a common denominator the yields on different bonds of differing maturity. My method reflects what you would receive *actually*, not theoretically.

In any event, I have demonstrated a no-risk way to earn both income and long-term capital gain in a security that threw off both kinds of yields—with perfect safety in the no-loss section of the money market game.

But if you bought this issue, which had more than 14 months to mature, chances are you bought it to make capital gains in the short-term because you expected interest rates to drop in 1981. If they didn't drop, as you projected at time of purchase, you might have to sell the holding out at a loss.

The Risky Bond/Note Game

If, after your August 18 purchase of the $100,000 note, interest rates dropped sharply during the last quarter of 1981, as so many experts predict, you might be able to resell at, say, 94 after holding it for only 90 days. How would this stack up against waiting the entire time until it matures?

You paid $90,438 and resold for $94,000, 90 days later. The short-term gain on the trade amounted to $3,562 on the $90,438 investment, or an annual return of what?

Theoretical annual return = \$3,562 × 4 = \$14,248

$$\frac{\$14{,}248 \times 100}{\$90{,}438} = 15.75\%$$

Only 15.75%? Please understand that this only represents the capital gain portion of tying up \$90,438 for 90 days. What about the interest? Wouldn't you be earning at the annual current yield of the 7.125% interest rate on the \$100,000 face value for which you paid only \$90,438? So to the annualized return of 15.75% you also have to add the annualized interest earned during the 90-day period. After you do this you'll find that the risky trade yielded 15.75% gain + 7.88% interest to total 22.63% return for the risk-taker, on an annual basis.

But how do you know which notes or bonds to buy? How do you know whether the short-term bonds will move faster in the direction of the interest-rate trend than the longer ones, or vice versa?

You have to make decisions based either on research that you do yourself or on research that other experts do for you that leads you to make a selection and an investment decision in the money market game.

Of course, there are the lessons of financial history that have generally repeated in the recurring inflation/deflation cycles that have beset our country since the Revolutionary War. But it is almost axiomatic that fluctuations in the general level of interest rates cause more significant fluctuations in long-term bond and note prices than they do in short-term. Historically, when interest rates rise, long-term bonds drop more sharply than short-term; and when interest rates fall, long-term bonds and notes rise faster in price than short-term. While both long and short-term government bonds and notes rise and fall in unison, they do this to differing degrees; and that's where the profits come in when you play the risky bond/note game.

Incidentally, if interest rates had risen during the 90-day holding period of the long-term note in the previous example, you could have sold out at a loss as the down-trend in interest set in (part of that loss would have been cushioned, of course, by the interest accrued) or you could have elected to hold until maturity in November 1982 and wound up without a loss but with a substantial long-term gain.

The growth of the government debt money market has spawned exchange trading in government debt instrument futures (T-bills, T-bonds, T-notes) and also trading in commercial paper and CD contracts for future delivery months and this has led to a speculation game.

The Speculator Money Game

In this market you can swing the price action of $1-million in T-bills for 90-day delivery, or $100,000 lots of T-bonds and T-notes. You can make highly leveraged killings if you happen to have entered the market on the right side of it and exited before your positions, which are highly leveraged, go against you. It does not take much of an adverse move in T-bill futures trading in $1 million contracts to wipe out the good faith margin deposit of $2,000 a contract, which is the exchange-required minimum.

But because this book is written for the smart investor who wants to play it safe by earning high rates with low risk, or as has been demonstrated in this chapter, with *no risk,* I am not going to delve into detailed strategies of making or losing large sums of money in the speculator-futures game.* Instead I do want to point out that if you

* Before you even consider taking the plunge in T-bill or T-note futures, I recommend that you read Mark Powers and David Vogel, *Inside the Financial Futures Markets,* John Wiley, (New York, 1981).

have large holdings of either long-term or short-term government debt, this can be "hedged" (insured against risk) by making offsetting (opposite) trades in the financial futures pits.

Do-It-Yourself Money Research

Prudence dictates that if you are going to become an active participant with big money in the government money market game, you should do some of your own research and make some friendships in that area. The first thing you should do is get to know experts in the particular securities that interested you. For example, if you are solely interested in governments, you would open a huge account at one of the 30 money market banks that are plugged into the Federal Reserve primary distribution desk peddling newly issued debt instruments continuously on behalf of Uncle Sam.

These banks all publish informative letters for the use of their customers. There are also some brokerage houses that deal almost exclusively in government securities, and they also publish material that will aid you in your money market research.

Basically, everyone in the money market follows interest rates—and their trends. The Federal Reserve publishes statistical information that is readily available on request. To give you a view of money market daily rate changes over a period of a month, for comparison purposes, here's a sample of that report:

Interest Rates
(Yields in percent per annum)

Daily 1981 June	Federal Funds	Comm. paper 3-mo. 3/	CDs sec. mkt. 3-month	U.S. Government Securities: Treasury bills 3/ 3-month	6-month	1-year	Treasury constant maturities 1-year	2-year	3-year	5-year	7-year	10-year	20-year	30-year
1	19.01	16.13	16.77	15.50	14.49	13.45	15.13	14.47	14.35	13.99	13.61	13.46	13.22	13.06
2	19.45	16.86	17.37	15.69	14.60	13.51	15.21	14.66	14.45	14.07	13.75	13.58	13.32	13.13
3	20.35	17.15	17.38	15.64	14.55	13.48	15.17	14.65	14.38	14.05	13.71	13.55	13.30	13.08
4	20.05	17.17	17.54	15.81	14.74	13.61	15.33	14.76	14.45	14.10	13.76	13.51	13.28	13.04
5	19.99	17.19	17.80	15.83	14.73	13.58	15.27	14.73	14.45	14.10	13.78	13.56	13.27	13.11
8	18.73	16.61	16.87	15.18	14.14	13.12	14.68	14.31	14.11	13.78	13.53	13.36	13.08	12.87
9	18.36	16.43	16.94	15.01	14.03	13.14	14.71	14.41	14.20	13.87	13.59	13.37	13.11	12.89
10	18.22	16.01	16.51	14.69	13.88	13.11	14.65	14.31	14.11	13.78	13.51	13.31	13.03	12.82
11	18.76	16.08	16.68	14.56	13.94	13.26	14.85	14.40	14.16	13.84	13.57	13.32	13.05	12.84
12	18.33	16.07	16.61	14.53	13.98	13.11	14.78	14.44	14.21	13.87	13.61	13.35	13.05	12.84
15	18.83	15.68	16.12	13.72	13.45	12.65	14.20	14.03	13.86	13.57	13.33	13.09	12.84	12.61
16	19.39	15.65	16.12	13.73	13.46	12.76	14.34	14.11	13.88	13.58	13.27	13.08	12.85	12.59
17	21.71	15.81	16.21	14.24	13.75	13.02	14.67	14.37	14.11	13.71	13.40	13.23	12.96	12.73
18	20.68	16.11	16.86	15.00	14.40	13.45	15.19	14.66	14.46	14.10	13.75	13.57	13.23	12.98
19	20.61	16.69	17.71	14.87	14.23	13.28	14.97	14.65	14.44	14.07	13.71	13.46	13.15	12.90
22	18.75	16.52	17.18	14.36	13.88	13.04	14.67	14.49	14.31	13.96	13.63	13.44	13.13	12.86
23	16.75	15.92	16.62	14.50	13.99	13.22	14.88	14.59	14.35	14.00	13.62	13.56	13.22	12.99
24	16.37	15.98	16.78	14.70	14.17	13.35	15.04	14.71	14.46	14.10	13.83	13.66	13.38	13.10
25	18.43	16.38	17.09	14.24	13.99	13.28	14.95	14.65	14.42	14.08	13.87	13.70	13.41	13.14
26	18.39	16.40	17.16	14.13	13.85	13.12	14.74	14.59	14.39	14.09	13.84	13.69	13.44	13.14
29	18.55	16.13	16.75	13.94	13.75	13.02	14.60	14.48	14.33	14.01	13.84	13.68	13.41	13.11
30	18.64	16.04	16.70	14.28	13.88	13.24	14.87	14.66	14.57	14.25	14.15	13.86	13.59	13.30

SOURCE: Federal Reserve Statistical Release G.13(415), July 6, 1981.

In addition to much statistical releases and quarterly reviews of the money situation in the United States, the Federal Reserve banks in twelve districts throughout the country publish explanatory material, statistical data, and critical commentary on monetary affairs. Practically *all* the information printed in the newspapers about money movements and asset sizes of financial companies comes from the data released daily and weekly by the Reserve Bank. And it's truly remarkable how accommodating the N.Y. Fed is if you visit its publication section, which is open to the public during business days.

The offerings from the group of secondary market government securities dealers who are linked to the N.Y. Fed appear, in part, in the daily press all over the country.

Of course, there are other published sources that dissect and analyze what's happening in the money market here and abroad. *The American Banker* and *The Financial Times* (of London) report daily. *Bondweek,* a publication of the *Institutional Investor,* provides weekly gossip and facts about all phases of the money market, including a weekly "Rate Roundup" such as the one that follows:

Rate Roundup

	Close 7/16	*Change from 7/9*
SHORT-TERM		
Fed funds	18.50	–1.50
Overnight repos	18.40	–0.60
30-day prime CDs	17.85	–0.85
30-day commercial paper	17.13	–0.87
90-day treasuries	14.54	–0.585
90-day prime CDs	17.60	–0.65
90-day commercial paper	16.75	–0.50
6-month treasuries	14.37	–0.355
12-month treasuries	13.61	–0.265
Prime bank lending rate	20.50	—
Telerate Money Market Index	16.50	–0.64

(continued)

	Close 7/16	Change from 7/9
	LONG-TERM	
Baa industrials	16.25	—
Baa utilities	17.125	+0.175
A industrials	15.00	−0.25
A utilities	16.20	—
Aa industrials	14.375	+0.125
Aa utilities	15.90	+0.05
Aaa industrials	13.95	+0.05
Bell System debentures	15.50	+0.26
10-year treasuries	14.14	−0.01
30-year treasuries	13.46	−1.01
Bond Buyer 20 Bond Index (munis)	11.09	+0.12
	YANKEE BONDS	
5-year	15.45	−0.05
8-year	15.50	−0.05
20-year	15.70	−0.05
	AGENCIES	
	Yield to maturity	*Change on week*
FHLB 7.375% 11/26/93	13.66	—
Fed'l Land Bank 7.95% 10/21/96	13.30	—
Fannie Mae 9.80% 10/10/91	14.26	+0.01
Ginnie Mae 8% (12-yr. average life)	14.63	+0.13

If I were giving out awards for financial reporting, which of course I am not in a position to do, I'd elect *The Financial Times* of London for the best source of money market analysis. During the week ending July 24, 1981, money markets displayed rather unusual volatility as Mr. Volcker appeared before Congress to warn that while inflation had improved he wasn't convinced we'd turned the corner. The analysis of that week's ups and downs by the *Financial Time*'s David Lascelles reflected one of the keenest reviews of the money markets I have ever read. And incidentally, I don't mind confessing that I use the

London *Financial Times* to help me make my own forecasting decisions. Because of that newspaper's innovative approach to both reporting and marketing, as well as printing, I'm able to read it in my New York office on the same morning it is published in Frankfurt, Germany, via telephone from London.

The way this modern miracle works is that the *Financial Times* is set in London, quipped by phone to Frankfurt, where the salmon-color newspapers are printed, and flown by Lufthansa to the U.S. Because of the six-hour time differential flying west from Frankfurt to the U.S., the newspapers arrive in New York early on the same morning they are printed in Germany. Messengers then hand-deliver the papers to New York subscribers. The annual subscription is about $400—but I could hardly do a day's work without it.

Another fine financial newspaper is the *Journal of Commerce.* Since most of that publication's clients are readers in various sectors of industry, assuredly they all have one common interest—what's going on in the world of short-term money. A lucid explanation of why volatility exists each week in short-term rates appeared in that newspaper's editorial column of July 20, 1981:

The Wednesday Scramble

BANKERS WILL TELL you that the Wednesday scramble to come up with funds to meet the reserve requirements levied by the Federal Reserve can be hair-raising. The problem may be intensified when the Fed, at the advice of the monetarists, eliminates the two-week lag in bank reserve requirements and switches to contemporaneous accounting, as is generally expected. The bidding for funds, which begins in earnest Tuesday, contributes to short-term volatility in the money markets. Last Wednesday, for example, the federal funds rate, the rate at which banks lend uncommitted reserves to each other, jumped from an encouraging 16 percent to a disheartening 30 percent. The scramble makes it difficult for the Fed to distinguish and respond to changes in operating factors, such as the float and money in circulation, from changes in demand for bank reserves.

Capricious and transitory movements in interest rates make it difficult for the Fed to keep the monetary aggregates in their target ranges and to restore them when they do break the bounds. The volatility also imposes severe costs on financial market participants, already breathless as a result of the Fed's switch in October 1979, to quantitative monetary control, who must cover themselves against wild movements in rates.

THE FED, with a good deal of encouragement from Morgan Guaranty Trust Co. and other members of the New York Clearing House, currently is taking a look at the possibility of adopting a four-week period for averaging bank reserves and staggering reserve settlements with one-fourth of the reporting banks, their numbers now swollen by foreign banks and other financial institutions, each week. This would allow temporary reserve supply aberrations to be spread out over a month's time.

The change would provide a major help to the banks in managing their money positions because they would not have to focus so much on the settlement date and worry more about the fundamental trend in interest rates and Fed policy. It would also reduce volatility in rates on a day-to-day basis. There is the danger, of course, that deficiencies and excesses in bank reserves could build up over time, contributing to greater swings in rates over extended periods.

From the Fed's point of view, the money desk would no longer have to guess at the level of float or the money in circulation and could wait a day to see what really happened to the money number. It could operate, therefore, from the real numbers rather than on the "market tone and feel."

The change would also reduce the need for banks to go to the discount window, because under the staggered approach three-quarters of the banks would always be in the position to offer funds to the other quarter at some price. This would enable the Fed to be more restrictive in its lending, forcing banks to correct reserve shortages by reducing the level of deposits. With total reserves and non-borrowed reserves coming more closely into line, the Fed could presumably substitute total reserves for non-borrowed reserves as the key policy instruments as the monetarists have also suggested.

Under the present system, the various district banks—which have differing guidelines on member bank borrowings and are subject to complaints about fairness and equity—are hard put to control bank borrowings to meet reserve requirements.

Volatility in interest rates imposes real and measurable costs on the real economy. Banks can no longer price their short-term loans on the basis of a prime rate calculated on the average cost of funds, and a whole series of specialized lending rates have emerged. The prime rate now applies strictly to long-term borrowers. Anything that will tie the cost of funds to the banks to more fundamental economic considerations and make the cost of loans to industry more predictable is worth serious debate and active consideration.

So what has this got to do with your making money in the money market through its trading games?

It's the *volatility* of interest rates that causes the price changes. If rates were stable, a lot of professionals handling billions of dollars daily in the exciting money market might be working as air traffic controllers. And because of this volatility you can make money fron the Wednesday "scramble" if you have correctly anticipated beforehand what's going to happen weekly at the N.Y. Fed. By entering the money market in short or long-term governments and exiting before the next Wednesday hassle, you may win. If you are wrong, you could wind up with short-term losses instead of profits.

10

Money Market Tax Tintinnabulations

No matter what else can be said about President Richard M. Nixon, it was during his administration that the tax law was amended so that a hard-working, honest American citizen who wanted to keep abreast of rising inflation by *earning* as much money as possible only had to share 50% with his governmental "partner," the Internal Revenue Service.

I repeat: *50% maximum on earned income.*

And even though Mr. Donoghue urges his subscribers to "make your money work as hard as you do," the result of making money in the money market by earning interest from money market debt instruments, or money fund dividends, or money market certificate interest at banks and thrifts—all of it—is *unearned income* (taxed at 70%).

Instead of seeking out every tax loophole to shelter my earnings and returns from savings and investments, I decided some time ago to make ends meet simply by *earning more money*. After Nixon, this made sense to me, since I only had to give half away, no matter how much money I made. But it didn't make any sense to me to enter into any risk ventures, since I'd have to give away the lion's share of my windfall if the risk turned profitable in a short period of time—and if it turned into a partial or total loss I could only offset my income by up to $3,000 in a tax year.

Risking large sums of money in money funds, however, does not come under the same considerations as other short-term risk ventures for the following reason: if I earn $14 on a $1,000 investment in a money fund in one month and give 70% to Uncle Sam, there's still $4.20 left. Now, if I earn $5 or so on the same amount in a month in a passbook bank or thrift account and have to contribute to our government on this at the 70% rate, what will I have left? You don't have to do advanced math to see that I'll wind up with $1.50 in the passbook account.

Tax-Free Funds

Understanding that intelligent people attempt to pay the least taxes legally possible on financial rewards, several fund managements have launched "tax-free money market funds." These funds are not completely tax free. They are only free of federal income tax. If you live and work in a high-tax state like New York and, compounding this, earn your money in New York City, there are two other hands on your wallet.

Two money funds are of interest in this regard: The T. Rowe Price Tax-Exempt Money Fund and the Nuveen Tax-Exempt Money Fund. The latter fund requires an initial investment of $25,000, while the former asks for only $1,000 as the initial risk.

On June 9, 1981, the T. Rowe Price Tax-Exempt Money Fund's annualized yield was 7.58%. To see how this fits into your income plans, here is a table that is revealing, to say the least:

What Must You Earn When Paying Uncle Sam to Match Tax-Free Yields?

Joint Return	*Single Return*	*Your maximum tax bracket*	*4%*	*5%*	*6%*	*7%*	*8%*
			To match a tax-free yield of: before paying uncle sam you must earn:				
$ 29,901– 35,200		37	6.35	7.94	9.52	11.11	12.70
‡$ 45,801– 60,000	$ 34,101–41,500	49	7.84	9.80	11.76	13.73	15.69
$ 85,601–109,400		59	9.76	12.20	14.63	17.07	19.51
$215,401 & over	$108,301 & over	70	13.33	16.67	20.00	23.33	26.67

‡ Net amount subject to Federal income tax after deductions and exemptions. Your zero bracket amount has been built into these Tax Rate Schedules. The maximum tax on earned income is 50%. Investment income may be taxed up to 70%.

* The yield quoted is based on the Fund's dividends for the seven days ended on the date indicated, and divided by the average of the daily net asset values per share of the Fund ($1.00) for such period. The yield should not be considered a representation of the yield of the Fund in the future. The Fund's yield is not fixed or guaranteed, and the principal value is not insured. This yield is higher than it normally would be since the Fund is currently not paying any advisory fee and Price Associates is currently assuming all expenses of the Fund. See Section, "Investment Adviser", of the Fund's Prospectus for full explanation regarding the phasing in of the advisory fee and assumption of the Fund's expenses by Price Associates. Income may be subject to state and local taxes.

This literature is authorized for distribution only to shareholders and to others who have received a copy of the prospectus of the Fund.

In the Nuveen Fund sales literature, the management stresses that depending on your tax bracket you could generate more *spendable* income with a tax-free money fund than with the yields available from taxable money funds. Here is their illustrative table:

Equivalent Taxable Yield Table (%)
Individual Income Brackets-(000)

Single return*		$34.1 to $41.5		$41.5 to $55.3		$55.3 to $81.8		$ 81.8 to $108.3	over $108.3
Joint return*		$45.8 to $60.0	$60.0 to $85.6		$ 85.6 to $109.4		$109.4 to $162.4	$162.4 to $215.4	over $215.4
%Tax bracket	TAX-EXEMPT YIELDS (%)	*49*	*54*	*55*	*59*	*63*	*64*	*68*	*70*
	4.00	7.84	8.70	8.89	9.76	10.81	11.11	12.50	13.33
	4.50	8.82	9.78	10.00	10.98	12.16	12.50	14.06	15.00
	5.00	9.80	10.87	11.11	12.20	13.51	13.89	15.63	16.67
	5.50	10.78	11.96	12.22	13.41	14.86	15.28	17.19	18.33
	6.00	11.76	13.04	13.33	14.63	16.22	16.67	18.75	20.00
	6.50	12.75	14.13	14.44	15.85	17.57	18.06	20.31	21.67
	7.00	13.73	15.22	15.56	17.07	18.92	19.44	21.88	23.33
	7.50	14.71	16.30	16.67	18.29	20.27	20.83	23.44	25.00
	8.00	15.69	17.39	17.78	19.51	21.62	22.22	25.00	26.67

*Net amount subject to federal income tax after deductions and exemptions.

As of July 22, 1981, the Nuveen Tax Exempt Money Market Fund had net assets of $78.7-million, with an average portfolio maturity of 64 days and an average 7-day yield of 7.20%. It contained 69% project notes, 5% tax-exempt commercial paper, 25% general obligation bonds and notes, and 1% revenue bonds.

The giant brokerage houses, of course, are intensely income-tax-conscious, and Merrill Lynch offers tax-free pooled investments, while Hutton offers Municipal Cash Reserve Management, a fund that invests "at least 80% of its net assets in short-term, tax-exempt obligations." Interestingly enough, the prospectus for this fine fund indicates that Hutton can "charge a shareholder's Hutton account through which fund shares are purchased $5 for each redemption (not to exceed, however, 2% of the net asset value of the shares redeemed) and $5 for semi-annual maintenance if such shareholder's account has not generated more than $100 in gross commission business with Hutton during the six-month period prior to the first day of the month during which any such redemption occurs or during which the semi-annual maintenance fee would be imposed."

Could this be regarded as a tie-in sale?

In any event, the current thrust of brokerage firms and mutual fund managements alike seems to be to maximize taxable yield in some funds while minimizing tax liability in others. You make your choice—and send money.

Ideally, a tax-free money market fund should have the following attributes:

1. Daily tax-exempt (federal) income
2. Monthly reinvestment or dividend check
3. $1-a-share constant net asset value
4. Average portfolio maturity under 120 days
5. No sales or redemption fees

What Hutton has done about fees in its Municipal Cash Reserve Fund is much less irksome than having to keep thousands of dollars in a non-interest-paying checking account as a "compensating balance" in order to get a decent loan in time of monetary tightness.

The T-Bill Tax Game

Before money funds came into prominence many people used to play the T-bill game. Some years ago T-bills were still issued in $10,000 and higher certificates of a bearer type. Thus they could be passed from one person to another without record. Moreover, the bills didn't pay interest; they just threw off face value on or after the maturity date—with the discount representing the gain in the form of income to the bearer, or holder, or owner.

The government claims it shifted into "book entry" sale of weekly bills at the auctions because of savings in cost. (No paper has to be issued or redeemed; the whole process involves entry into a computer or "book.")

But some doubting Thomases believe the government resorted to computerized bookkeeping because people were evading payment of taxes on the earnings from the T-bills bought at discount.

Incidentally, by some unexplained rationale, T-bills are considered *nonfinancial instruments*. Thus, at this writing, a person who buys T-bills and sells them at a loss can deduct the entire loss from income. At the same time there can be no capital-gains treatment on these bills because any gains in resale or at maturity is income. Oddly enough, all other government obligations throwing off interest income can be bought and sold for capital gains and losses if not held to maturity.

All the other money market debt instruments are *securities*. Purchases and sales, gains and losses, income from interest or yield on discounted items are covered under the tax code pertaining to securities. Since the major portion of money market debt instruments traded in the market place are short-term (30 to 90 days), reselling any such securities before maturity will result in short-term gain or loss, as the case may be.

So the next time your broker who knows you have $50,000 in his firm's money fund account calls you and whispers, "I can get you a 30-day Manny-Hanny [for Manufacturers Hanover Trust] CD for 18%," you'd better examine your tax situation. Moreover, use the money market math you've learned to determine whether 18% simple interest for one month is better than 17.8% compounded daily for the same period in the money fund.

The Interest-Free Play

Now you may happen to be in the 50% income bracket, (70% unearned income) but other members of your family probably are not. For example, if you have a son or daughter attending a college and you want to cushion the rising costs of a college education by decreasing your tax liability on yields at your money fund, you can make an interest-free family loan to your offspring by opening up a money fund account in his or her name, and the offspring pays taxes on the dividends received.

This could be a substantial savings of tax payment by the parent and thus an increase in the net thrown off by the fund to the official shareholder. There is a distinct possibility that such loans may be challenged by the IRS, if not scrutinized, but currently this tax treatment is limited to interest-free demand loans with no fixed term, enforceable under state law.

You can also shift money to help a child buy a home or to finance the startup of a business—just as long as the money is a loan and not a gift, and the recipient pays the taxes on any tangible benefits therefrom.

Set Up an IRA

Prior to the fall of 1981, any person covered by pension or profit-sharing plans at regular employment was barred from establishing an IRA (individual retirement account) at a bank, thrift, or at a mutual fund through a stockbroker or directly.

But the passage of a bill just before the summer 1981 congressional recess enables any employee to set up an IRA and shelter specific amounts of money each year. The funds have to be withdrawn between the ages of 59½ and 70, and arrangements can be made to withdraw the monies in a lump sum when the shelter ends or to draw monthly sums, permitting the balance to remain sheltered.

The inherent beauty of such a device as IRA is that the contributions by the taxpayer are a *deduction* from income and the compounded interest or dividends are tax free until withdrawn.

Assume that you are in the 30% bracket and set up an IRA permitting you to contribute to a plan formalized with a bank, a broker, a money fund, a thrift, or a savings bank. You contribute the maximum permissible amount, $2,000. Then your tax liability that year will be reduced by $600 (30% of $2,000).

Your contribution, therefore, is deducted from gross income, and, unlike a contribution to a charity, your contribution remains your money.

The potential market represented by the more than 40 million employables who can benefit from establishing IRAs has banks, thrifts, brokers, and money fund managements drooling at their ad agencies, as campaigns are being readied to ensnare the flood of dollars going into IRA after January 1, 1982.

Of course, we don't know where interest rates will be on January 1, 1982, but if past performance continues—and no restrictions are saddled on the money-making power of money funds—potential contributors to new IRA plans won't find it too hard to decide whether they should shelter their retirement money at bank rates or at money fund dividend levels.

Remember: basically, the earnings you will receive (outside shelters like funds in IRA or Keogh Plans) from investments in either money market instruments, where you will receive interest, or money funds, where you receive dividends, are all *unearned income* and are taxed that way.

It could well be that there will be a new wave of money funds of a tax-free nature. But none of them could ever have my money. I have seen what they invest in and there's no way in the world to convince me that *any* municipal bond, whether it be general obligation, revenue, or industrial development will be other than category X in my book, which means "avoid or switch." I do make one exception, and that is in New York State School District Bonds, which I happen to own in a modest amount. These obligations on a school district in Nassau County are not only backed by full faith but are also a lien on the real property of the taxpayers residing within the boundaries of the school district in event of default. These are the *only* safe municipal bonds I'd ever buy. But bonds are a long-term investment and subject to risk while they are in a portfolio. That is why I am not going to go into detail regarding municipal bonds, tax-free trusts, partnerships, and units. If you insist on investing in municipals and want professionally prepared management to assist you, try tax-free money funds—but remember *I rate them all with a great big X* for non-safety.

11

Making It in the Money Wars

The July 2, 1981, issue of *Newsday,* a newspaper widely distributed on Long Island, was one of the fattest single issues I've ever seen. It ran 200 pages. And it seemed to me that every third or fourth page was a full-page advertisement for a bank, savings bank, or savings and loan association offering to give something away in return for new deposits.

The fact is that competition from money funds during the first half of 1981 drew billions of dollars of savings from traditional insured depositories such as banks and thrifts (I am considering savings banks and savings and loan associations under the single classification "thrifts").

In addition to the fact that money funds were paying out better yields—with no penalties for withdrawals—much publicity appeared in the press about losses being incurred at these banks and thrifts all over the country because of restrictive ceilings on passbook accounts and certificate accounts—with the exception of the T-bill-rate bank money market certificate accounts.

And then—because our country's monetary system has traditionally been based on the supply of funds for business, private construction, and essential needs—the government came to the aid of the banks so that they could compete with money funds for both savings and reserve funds. But before going on to examine how the banks and thrifts are now competing with the aggressive advertising of the money funds, I'll try to explain precisely what banks and thrifts really are.

Meet the Banks

Commercial banks, professionally known simply as "banks," primarily serve businesses as safe harbors for cash flow, checking accounts, and sources of credit lines and loans. Every business in America today runs on some form of credit, and commercial banks loom large in planning for cash to meet short, intermediate- and long-term financing for all types of businesses. Savings accounts have always been of secondary consideration in commercial banking, while service of business needs was primary.

In addition, banks serve their stockholders by taking risk activity in the government securities market (approved dealers at the Federal Reserve include giant "money market banks" such as Chase, Citibank, and Continental of Illinois) and also earn money by raising capital as agents for commercial corporations in the short-term money market. For example, on July 15, 1981, Chase Manhattan Bank ran a full-page advertisement in *The Wall Street Journal* that told the world it had taken Chase only 23 hours from request to delivery to gather up $100 million "to help a multi-national oil company avoid a cash flow problem" (the commission the bank earned in this deal, of course, was not publicized). Then the ad went on to boast that it had taken the bank only 2 hours to arrange a multimillion stock repurchase for a customer.

Most of the 14,000-odd commercial banks in the United States are members of the Federal Reserve Board. But there are also state-chartered commercial banks that have chosen to remain nonmembers.

Business around our country and indeed around the world, understands the need for and the use of commercial banks; and sufficiently flexible rules have been laid down by the Federal Reserve Board to permit these banks to engage in international money-making activity, whatever the level of interest rates happens to be.

Meet the Thrifts

Traditional savings depositories, whose basic functions involved offering a safe storage place for people's and businesses savings and providing loans for private housing came to be known as "thrifts." Basically, there are three classes of thrifts: savings banks; savings and loan associations; and credit unions. Because the bulk of people's savings used to lie in reserve at mutual savings banks and at savings and loan associations, I will not go into detail about credit unions. But I am going to dwell a bit on the other two categories of traditional insured depositories.

Mutual savings banks, professionally known as savings institutions, had their origins in the eighteenth century. In some savings banks, a person could at one time open an account with a 5¢ or 10¢ deposit. That is why some of them still have those amounts in their name—for example, the 5¢ Savings Bank in New England and the Dime Savings Bank in New York. The primary purpose of these banks was to encourage Americans to save a little bit out of their pay every week, so that people would get to know that the interest earned from savings would make their nest eggs grow and grow. Today these savings banks, which are allegedly owned "mutually" by the depositors, still offer passbook savings accounts insured up to $100,000 per account, from which funds can be withdrawn at any time without penalty. The nature of these deposits is generally short-term. But the lending activities of savings banks has traditionally been long term, limited to such things as housing mortgages and home improvement loans. Thus, in years past, if passbook accounts received 5¼% per annum dividends, home mortgages supplied by the savings banks with the depositors' monies would run at, say, 7½%. And while the deposits that purchased these mortgages might flow in and out of these institutions during brief periods of time, the mortgages might run for 25 years and more. Understandably, then, savings banks could hardly exist very long if they were compelled to pay interest to depositors at rates higher than the return on their mortgage portfolios.

Savings and loan associations, which today number over 4,000, were founded in the nineteenth century when people needed money to build or buy homes but could not get the funds from the savings banks. Chartered by the various states, the savings and loan associations at first were restricted to lending activity in their own locale. These associations over the years have found themselves more and more restricted from competing with either banks or savings institutions. And in the meantime, commercial banks began to make competitive inroads on what was formerly the principal province of the thrifts and savings banks.

As a result, by the summer of 1981, the lines of deposit and loan activity had become increasingly blurred, with little sign of regulatory remonstrance from agencies charged with supervision. That is why I became rather annoyed when I walked into my savings bank recently and saw a sign that invited depositors to inquire about personal and auto loans. I had always thought personal and auto loans were the proper province of commercial banks. As I drove down the highway one afternoon on the way home I noticed a giant sign over a thrift that invited me to "bank by car." And my wife has money in a thrift association that has a huge sign in the lobby advising depositors of its "banking hours."

It is no wonder that people have come to think of money funds as bank substitutes. If they can be misled to the effect that a thrift has "banking hours" and that a savings bank is the place to go to get an auto loan, who can fault people for believing they are getting daily "interest" on their share accounts at the money funds?

But believe me, the problems at the thrifts did not wholly arise from people moving passbook deposits out and placing them in shares of better-paying money funds. The key problem of borrowing short (from depositors) and being unable to profit from lending long (to builders and home buyers) hurt the thrifts badly during 1979 and 1980. In 1981, when interest rates soared to record highs and operational losses loomed among the ranks of the previously prosperous thrifts, they had to get help—and they did—from the government.

The Deregulation Gambit

Under regulations adopted on June 25 and effective August 1, 1981, via the good graces of the Depository Institutions Deregulation Committee, banks and thrifts were permitted to raise rates on 30-month small savers certificates to the average yield of 30-month Treasury notes. The former certificate ceiling of 12% for four-year deposits still remained in effect. So at least thrifts and commercial banks were in a little better position to battle the money funds for the savers' dollars.

The next significant piece of help for the banks and thrifts came when Congress passed President Reagan's economic program of budget cuts and tax cuts just before the August recess. Part of this bill created a magnificent marketing tool for the traditional depositories in the form of the new All-Savers certificates, available October 1, 1981. What it does is to make it possible for citizens to invest for one year in these certificates, which will be pegged at 70% of the going one-year T-bill rate. The investors will be able to deposit as little as $1,000 and receive tax-free interest up to $1,000 per person if single or $2,000 per couple if married.

Now the guns of August in the money wars of 1981 began to blast away in newspaper advertisements. By mid-August, deal after deal was being offered to the saving public to open up accounts at banks and thrifts that would pay anywhere from 18% to 29.41% for the 40 days or so from the date of the ad until September 30, and then on October 1 would be automatically converted *(principal and interest)* into a 12-month All-Saver certificate at the "highest yield allowed by law."

Of course, because the 40-day certificate paying you anywhere from 18% to 29.4%—depending on how much of a cash bonus went along with your deposit—was simply a *repurchase agreement,* while the thrift would sell you a repo paying a high annualized yield for 40 days and then buy its certificate back, locking up your money at substantially lower interest costs for one year (or else you pay a penalty), the first 40 days of this ploy would be uninsured. But after your money was deposited on October 1 in an All-Saver, it would be insured.

All-Saver Certificate Analysis

I fished out a stub of a pencil and did some figuring. The ads for All-Savers certificates made them look like the greatest way a husband and wife could shelter $2,000 of income for the coming tax year. But when I began to examine all the facets, doubts crept in.

1. The certificate benefits only taxpayers in the over-30% bracket.
2. There was no guarantee as to what the one year T-bill rate would be on October 1.
3. To receive the $2,000 tax exemption from the joint-account interest earned, it would take an investment of about $20,000 at anticipated annual yield on 70% of the anticipated one year bill rate.
4. I couldn't help but ask myself why people would want to lock up $1,000 to $5,000 under such cir-

cumstances. An investment of $1,000 yielding 18% for 40 days and then getting about $100 worth of the permissible tax exemption simply doesn't make money management sense to me.

5. Earnings for six months on a regular bank money market certificate maturing in mid-February 1982 are well above 16% on an annualized basis. Why lock up funds at 70% of a rate that might be 18% in October 1981, when one can earn over 16% before taxes—and without any exemption? If the one-year T-bill rate were 18% in October, the rate at which the All-Saver would be locked in for a year could be 12.6%, simple interest—and not compounded daily or quarterly.
6. Finally, the fine print informs us that FDIC requires substantial penalties on premature withdrawal—a penalty that would be charged if the All-Saver account was not opened on October 1.

So, as you can see, investors could act in August and even get a cash bonus; but if they didn't lock up their deposits for another year from October 1, then they would have to give back the cash and probably most if not all of the 40-day interest headlined in the ad that drew them to the specific bank or thrift to begin with.

As for me, I decided to wait until October 1 and see what the rates were then.

Money-War Benefits

Now, while the money wars heat up between the banks and thrifts and the money funds competing in the media for your savings and cash reserves, here are some benefits you may derive from banks and thrifts:

1. *Revise your passbook and checking accounts:* Make sure your accounts for savings are day of deposit to

day of withdrawal. If you do not have such an account, *simply switch.* If your checking account does not throw off interest on the unused balance, make sure you arrange for it to earn money for you or else take the account out and put it in a bank or thrift that will pay for the use of your money.

2. *Consolidate passbook trust accounts:* If you hold a lot of small accounts in trust for family members, simply designate them as sharing in a single account that could earn triple the passbook rate at the same savings institution or bank in a certificate account.
3. *Get monthly interest if you can on bank certificates:* When savings institutions and banks began to issue money market certificates, they paid the interest in one lump sum on the date the certificate matured. Competition compelled many of them to offer monthly shifting of interest earned to a passbook account so it could compound at 5½%. There also was an option—one I religiously use in all my certificate accounts—and that is the bank would mail the monthly interest to me. In this way, if I have a certificate account for 26 weeks, I receive six interest checks, one a month. Where do these monthly checks go? Right into the brokerage account to be converted into new money fund shares the very same day and to be compounded daily thereafter. I suggest that before you renew or invest in a money market certificate, you arrange to have your interest sent monthly to you instead of having it deposited in your passbook account.
4. *Assess all exceptionally high interest deals carefully:* One of the opening guns in the summer 1981 money war was a full-page ad on July 20 by an aggressive New York commercial bank offering 20% simple interest for 66 months (5½ years) and an expensive wristwatch to boot. Setting aside the value of

the watch, here's what I found upon assessment of this deal that would lock in my money for 5½ years at 20%:

End year 1: Investment $10,000
Interest @ 20%: $2,000
End year 2: Investment $12,000 + $2,000
Interest on $10,000 = $2,000
End year 3: Investment $14,000 + $2,000
Interest on $10,000 = $2,000
End year 4: Investment $16,000 + $2,000
Interest on $10,000 = $2,000
End year 5: Investment $18,000 + $2,000
Interest on $10,000 = $2,000
End year 5½: Investment $20,000 + $1,000
Interest six months on $10,000 = $2,000
End year 1: Bank paid 20% on my equity of $10,000 + $2,000 earned interest
End year 2: Bank paid 20% on $10,000 of my $14,000 equity
End year 3: Bank paid 20% on $10,000 of my $16,000 equity
End year 4: Bank paid 20% on $10,000 of my $18,000 equity
End year 5: Bank paid 20% on $10,000 of my $20,000 equity
End year 5½: Bank paid 10% on my $20,000 equity

The bank, of course, will pay 20% per annum simple interest for the next 5½ years on the original investment of $10,000. But since the depositor cannot withdraw the earned interest each year, the bank is working with funds it doesn't have to pay interest on. The bank begins the account at the 20% annual rate and winds up the last six months paying half that rate on the equity. This 20% simple rate would equal a 14.44% rate for the same period of time if compounded quarterly.

5. Many advertised deals for your money include a cash bonus up front. The thrift advertising 29.41% for 40 days to entice depositors to its All-Savers account offered a 1¼% cash bonus for deposits from $2,500 to $25,000. The $2,500 deposit bonus was $31.25; the $25,000 one $312.50. How much will the IRS get out of the bonus?
   What I'm trying to say is, don't go for the bait unless you want to get hooked like a lot of other investors who may not be smart enough to weigh the risks and rewards of any deal that sounds almost too good to be true and carries a gift of cash with it.
6. Finally, the same innovative bank that thought up the 20%-5½-year simple interest method of locking in $10,000 at actual 14.44% compounded rates jumped headlong into the fray, seeking large depositors with a $100,000 "Money Market Account." The ad asked what money fund offered the best daily yield, easy access, and FDIC insurance. And in answer to these desirable attributes, the bank offered to take charge of $100,000—with no charge for withdrawal if the depositor gave 14 days' notice. In return the reward for depositors would be the average of the daily rate of three money funds: Merrill Ready Assets, Fidelity Daily Income, and Dreyfus Liquid Assets. Since the account would be insured, and money funds are not insured, the bank offers the money fund shareholder with $100,000 the *security* that *cannot be had with any money fund.*

I hope I have given you some direction as to the benefits on hand as the war for your money heats up. Furthermore, I hope I have provided sufficient background for you to understand how to be a smart investor in this struggle for your dollars.

In the meantime, there is a distinct possibility that you will be able to learn—and earn—as you investigate the ongoing competition between banks and thrifts and money funds. Perhaps from this strenuous struggle for survival between traditional depositories and the money funds may emerge conditions that will enable you to work your money satisfactorily on both sides of the scene to reap future rewards. A glimmer of hope in this direction arose in mid-August when a thrift advertised in *The Wall Street Journal* an invitation for deposits into an "insured asset growth fund": as little as $1,000 invested; yield changes daily, tied to average daily weighted yield on money market instruments; no withdrawal penalty; free check writing ($500 or more); dividends compounded daily (credited monthly); additional deposits accepted any time; insured to $100,000 per account by an agency of the state of Maryland. The advertised yield for August 4 was 19.23%. I wonder how long it takes a check on this hybrid to clear?

As for me, after working for a half-century, raising a fine family, and paying my taxes each year without too much grumbling, I cannot take the time to figure where all the money I ever made went. Not knowing where your money went is quite excusable and totally understandable. But, *only you can control where it is now—and where it will go and grow in the future.* Good luck!

Epilogue

As this book goes to press, a new and better day is dawning for smart savers.

Congress has seen the merits of permitting employables to arrange their own retirement plans, in addition to any plans their employers already provide. Deregulation plans on the drawing boards will eventually hike passbook interest rates at banks and thrifts to levels much higher than in the past—and ceilings will be removed from bank and thrift certificate accounts. The new All-Savers certificate accounts that will be partially tax sheltered will attract new money to thrifts and savings banks. Mortgages of a variable nature will help these institutions grow and provide funds for new and existing housing. Smart savers will be able to arrange for their loved ones to keep most or all of their estates when they die.

And inflation?

According to government sources, we are on the threshold of deflation, where a penny saved isn't a penny lost any more.

Smart savers, therefore, will have new opportunities to multiply reserve funds—before, during, and after taxation.

As for the short-term money market, companies and governments at all levels (federal, state, and municipal) will have to resort continually to borrowing in order to roll over debt that will never be actually reduced or paid off. In similar manner, corporate borrowings should continue—especially if the prime rate remains high. I believe, as others do, that the short-term money market will keep on growing, no matter what level interest rates rise or fall to, because it's the kind of market that *breeds on itself*.

Money funds?

If the government doesn't hamper them seriously with non-interest-paying reserves, as it did some years ago, the money funds are here to stay *and grow*. If the funds ever begin to pay less than banks and thrifts, smart savers can always switch—speedily—by check, phone, or wire transfer.

In the meantime, remember to place your money where it does you the most good with the least overt risk. Sensible multiplication of ready cash reserves should be the name of the new money game of the eighties.

Appendix A

Money Fund Listings and Ratings

The safety and yield ratings that follow are based upon personally devised factors relating to portfolio content and performance of the funds rated as of July 8, 1981. While all the funds rated may be considered low risk for investment purposes, the various degrees of safety in the ratings used simply provide a measure for analysis.

1	2	3	4	5	6	7	8	9
Class	*Fund*	*AFF*	*MIN CK*	*SAF*	*YLD*	*INIT*	*ADD*	*EXP*

Explanation of the Columns

1. Reflects whether fund shares available are to private investors (P) or to institutional investors only (I). Thus the heading CLASS.
2. Fund name, address, and phone numbers under heading FUND.*
3. (AFF stands for) Sponsorship (affiliation) of fund: M, mutual investment company; I, insurance company; B, stockbrokerage company.
4. MIN CK refers to funds that offer check writing and

* Information supplied in this fund directory is as of August 1, 1981, courtesy ICI.

the size of the minimum check permitted to be drawn.

5. SAF stands for the portfolio safety rating designed by the author: G, best rating, PG, next best; R, risky; X, avoid or switch.**
6. YLD stands for the portfolio yield rating designed by the author: G, best rating, PG, next best; R, risky; X, avoid or switch; NR, not rated.**
7. INIT means the minimum size of the initial investment acceptable by described fund.
8. ADD stands for the minimum additional sum that can be used to purchase fund shares by the shareholder after opening a fund account.
9. EXP means expedited purchase or liquidation services: T, phone liquidation services; W, wire receipt and transfer; NR, not reported.

Class	*Fund*	*AFF*	*MIN CK*	*SAF*	*YLD*	*INIT*	*ADD*	*EXP*
I	Alliance Capital Reserves 140 Broadway New York, NY 10005 212/437-2121 800/221-5672 (toll-free)	B	$500	R	PG	$0	$0	T,W
I	Alliance Government Reserves 140 Broadway New York, NY 10005 212/437-2121	B	500	NR	NR	0	0	T,W
P	American General Reserve Fund, Inc. 2777 Allen Parkway P. O. Box 3247 Houston, TX 77001 713/522-1111 800/421-5666 (toll-free)	M	500	R	G	1,000	100	T, W

** Safety and yield ratings are as of July 8, 1981. Wherever information requested was not supplied by the fund, NR is used to indicate not reported. Thus, for those funds, it was not possible to provide a rating for safety and yield, and NR is used to indicate not rated.

Class Fund	AFF	MIN CK	SAF	YLD	INIT	ADD	EXP
P American Liquid Trust 99 High Street P.O. Box 1311 Boston, MA 02104 617/338-3200 800/225-1587 (toll-free)	M	500	PG	PG	10,000	0	T, W
P Boston Company Cash Management Portfolio One Boston Place Boston, MA 02106 617/722-7200 617/722-7250 (collect, MA only) 800/343-6324	M	500	R	G	2,500	100	T, W
P Capital Preservation Fund, Inc. 755 Page Mill Road Palo Alto, CA 94304 415/858-2400 800/982-6150 (toll-free, CA only) 800/227-8380 (toll-free)	M	500	G	PG	1,000	0	T, W
P Capital Preservation Fund II, Inc. 755 Page Mill Road Palo Alto, CA 94304 415/858-2400 800/982-6150 (toll-free, CA only) 800/227-8380 (toll-free)	M	500	G	G	1,000	0	T, W
P Cardinal Government Securities Trust 155 East Broad Street Columbus, OH 43215 614/464-6985 800/282-9446 (toll-free, OH only) 800/848-7734 (toll-free)	M	500	G	PG	2,500	500	NR
P Carnegie Government Securities Fund, Inc. 831 National City Bank Bldg. Cleveland, OH 44114 216/781-4440 800/232-2321 (toll-free)	M	500	NR	NR	1,000	500	NR
P Cash Equivalent Fund, Inc. 120 S. LaSalle Street Chicago, IL 60603 312/781-1121 800/621-1048 (toll-free)	B	500	X	G	1,000	100	T, W
P Cash Management Trust of America 333 South Hope Street Los Angeles, CA 90071 213/486-9200 800/421-8791 (toll-free)	M	500	R	G	5,000	50	T, W

Class	Fund	AFF	MIN CK	SAF	YLD	INIT	ADD	EXP
P	Centennial Capital Cash Management Trust One New York Plaza New York, NY 10004 212/825-4000 800/221-5833 (toll-free)	M	500	NR	NR	1,000	0	T, W
P	CMA Money Trust 165 Broadway One Liberty Plaza New York, NY 10080 212/637-6300 800/631-0749 (toll-free)	B	0	PG	G	20,000	1,000	T,W
P	Colonial Money Market Trust 75 Federal Street Boston, MA 02110 617/426-3750 800/225-2365 (toll-free)	M	NR	NR	NR	3,000	100	NR
P	Columbia Daily Income Company 521 S.W. Morrison Portland, OR 97205 503/222-3600 800/547-1037 (toll-free)	M	500	R	PG	1,000	500	T, W
P	Composite Cash Management Company 4th Floor S & E Building Spokane, WA 99201 509/624-4101	M	500	R	G	1,000	500	NR
P	Current Interest, Inc. Suite 4300 333 Clay Street Houston, TX 77002 713/751-2400	B	500	R	G	1,000	100	T, W
P	Daily Cash Accumulation Fund, Inc. 3600 South Yosemite P.O. Box 5061 Denver, CO 80217 303/770-2345 800/525-9310 (toll-free)	B	500	R	G	2,500	100	T, W
P	Daily Income Fund, Inc. 230 Park Avenue New York, NY 10169 212/697-8088	B	500	PG	PG	5,000	100	T, W

Class	Fund	AFF	MIN CK	SAF	YLD	INIT	ADD	EXP
P	Delaware Cash Reserve, Inc. Seven Penn Center Plaza (1,000/25) Philadelphia, PA 19103 215/988-1200 800/523-4640 (toll-free)	M	500	R	G	1,000	25	T, W
I	Dreyfus Government Series 767 Fifth Avenue New York, NY 10153 212/935-3000 800/223-5525 (toll-free)	M	500	G	PG	25,000	0	T, W
P	Dreyfus Liquid Assets, Inc. 767 Fifth Avenue New York, NY 10153 212/935-3000 800/223-5525 (toll-free)	M	500	R	G	2,500	100	T, W
I	Dreyfus Money Market Instruments, Inc. 767 Fifth Avenue New York, NY 10153 212/935-3000 800/223-5525 (toll-free)	M	500	NR	NR	50,000	100	T, W
P	Eaton & Howard Cash Management Fund 24 Federal Street Boston, MA 02110 617/482-8260 800/225-6265 (toll-free)	M	500	R	G	1,000	0	T, W
P	Edward D. Jones & Co. Daily Passport Cash Trust 421 Seventh Avenue Pittsburgh, PA 15219 412/288-1900 800/245-2442 (toll-free)	B	500	NR	NR	5,000	100	NR
P	Equitable Money Market Account, Inc. 35th Floor 767 Fifth Avenue New York, NY 10153 212/245-7333 800/442-8195 (toll-free, NY only) 800/223-0970	I	500	R	PG	2,500	100	T, W
P	FBL Money Market Fund, Inc. 5400 University Avenue West Des Moines, IA 50265 515/225-5400 800/422-3175 (toll-free, IA only) 800/247-4170 (toll-free)	M	500	NR	NR	1,500	100	NR

Class	Fund	AFF	MIN CK	SAF	YLD	INIT	ADD	EXP
I	Federated Master Trust 421 Seventh Avenue Pittsburgh, PA 15219 412/288-1900 800/245-2442 (toll-free)	M	0	NR	NR	100,000	0	T, W
P	Fidelity Cash Reserves 82 Devonshire Street Boston, MA 02109 617/726-0200 800/225-6190 (toll-free)	M	500	R	G	1,000	250	T, W
P	Fidelity Daily Income Trust 82 Devonshire Street Boston, MA 02109 617/726-0200 800/225-6190 (toll-free)	M	500	PG	PG	10,000	500	T, W
I	Fidelity Money Market Trust Domestic Portfolio U.S. Government Portfolio U.S. Dollar Denominated Money Market Portfolio U.S. Treasury Portfolio 82 Devonshire Street Boston, MA 02109 617/726-0200 800/225-6190 (toll-free)	M	0	NR	NR	250,000	0	T, W
P	First Investors Cash Management, Inc. 120 Wall Street New York, NY 10005 212/825-7900	M	500	G	G	1,000	100	T, W
P	First Variable Rate Fund for Government Income, Inc. 2301 Calvert Street, N.W. Washington, D.C. 20008 202/328-4000 800/424-2444 (toll-free)	M	500	G	PG	1,000	250	T, W
P	Florida Mutual U.S. Government Securities Portfolio I One Financial Plaza Suite 1507 Ft. Lauderdale, FL 33394 305/522-0200 800/432-1592 (toll-free, FL only)	I	NR	NR	NR	1,000	100	NR
P	Franklin Federal Money Fund 155 Bovet Road San Mateo, CA 94402 415/574-8800 800/227-6781 (toll-free)	M	500	G	PG	500	100	T, W

Class	Fund	AFF	MIN CK	SAF	YLD	INIT	ADD	EXP
P	Franklin Money Fund, Inc. 155 Bovet Road San Mateo, CA 94402 415/574-8800 800/227-6781 (toll-free)	M	500	PG	PG	500	100	T, W
P	Government Investors Trust 1800 North Kent Street Arlington, VA 22209 703/528-6500 800/336-3063 (toll-free)	M	500	G	G	2,000	0	T, W
P	Gradison Cash Reserves, Inc. 580 Building Cincinnati, OH 45202 513/579-5700 800/582-7062 (toll-free, OH only) 800/543-1818 (toll-free)	B	500	R	G	1,000	50	T, W
P	IDS Cash Management Fund, Inc. 1000 Roanoke Building Minneapolis, MN 55402 612/372-3131 800/328-8300 (toll-free)	M	500	R	PG	2,500	100	W
P	INA Cash Fund 3 Parkway, 11th Floor P.O. Box 7728 Philadelphia, PA 19101 215/241-2723 800/441-7786 (toll-free)	I	250	R	G	2,500	500	T, W
P	InterCapital Liquid Asset Fund Inc. Five World Trade Center New York, NY 10048 212/938-4500 800/221-2685 (toll-free)	B	500	R	PG	5,000	100	T, W
P	John Hancock Cash Management Trust John Hancock Place P.O. Box 111 Boston, MA 02117 617/421-6320 800/343-7180 (toll-free)	I	250	R	PG	1,000	25	T, W
P	Kemper Money Market Fund, Inc. 120 S. LaSalle Street Chicago, IL 60603 312/781-1121 800/781-1121 (toll-free)	I	500	X	PG	1,000	100	T, W

Class	Fund	AFF	MIN CK	SAF	YLD	INIT	ADD	EXP
P	Legg Mason Cash Reserve Trust 421 Seventh Avenue Pittsburgh, PA 15219 412/288-1900 800/245-2442 (toll-free)	B	500	R	PG	5,000	500	T, W
P	Lehman Cash Management 55 Water Street New York, NY 10041 212/558-2020 800/221-5350 (toll-free)	B	500	R	PG	5,000	250	T, W
P	Lexington Money Market Trust 580 Sylvan Avenue P.O. Box 1515 Englewood Cliffs, NJ 07632 201/567-2000 800/526-4791 (toll-free)		250	X	G	1,000	100	T, W
P	Liquid Capital Income, Inc. 831 National City Bank Building Cleveland, Ohio 44114 216/781-4440 800/321-2321 (toll-free)	B	500	R	G	1,000	500	T, W
I	Liquid Cash Trust 421 Seventh Avenue Pittsburgh, PA 15219 412/288-1900 800/245-2442 (toll-free)	M	NR	NR	NR	NR	NR	NR
P	Liquid Green Trust 207 Guaranty Building Indianapolis, IN 46204 317/634-3300 800/428-4492 (toll-free)	M	NR	NR	NR	1,000	500	NR
P	Lord Abbett Cash Reserve Fund, Inc. 63 Wall Street New York, NY 10005 212/425-8720 800/221-9995 (toll-free)	M	500	PG	G	1,000	0	T, W
P	Lutheran Brotherhood Money Fund, Inc. 421 Seventh Avenue Pittsburgh, PA 15219 412/288-1900 800/245-2442 (toll-free)	M	NR	NR	NR	2,500	100	NR
P	Massachusetts Cash Management Trust 200 Berkeley Street Boston, MA 02116 617/423-3500	M	500	R	G	1,000	0	T, W

Class Fund	AFF	MIN CK	SAF	YLD	INIT	ADD	EXP
I Master Reserves Trust Bank I Government Portfolio Bank I Money Market Portfolio Baybank Money Market Portfolio Baybank Short Term U.S. Government Portfolio Key Trust Money Market Portfolio Key Trust Government Portfolio Government Portfolio Hospital Trust Money Market Fund Money Market Portfolio 99 High Street, 32nd Floor Boston, MA 02104 617/338-3200 800/225-1587 (toll-free)	M	NR	NR	NR	NR	NR	NR
P Merrill Lynch Government Fund, Inc. 165 Broadway One Liberty Plaza New York, NY 10080 212/637-6300 800/631-0749 (toll-free)	B	500	G	PG	5,000	100	T, W
I Merrill Lynch Institutional Fund, Inc. 165 Broadway One Liberty Plaza New York, NY 10080 212/637-6300 800/631-0749 (toll-free)	B	500	PG	G	25,000	1,000	T, W
P Merrill Lynch Ready Assets Trust 165 Broadway One Liberty Plaza New York, NY 10080 212/637-6300 800/631-0749 (toll-free)	B	500	PG	PG	5,000	1,000	T, W
P Midwest Income Investment Company 508 Dixie Terminal Bldg. Cincinnati, OH 45202 513/579-0414 800/543-0407 (toll-free)	M	350	G	R	500	50	T, W
P MIF/Nationwide Money Market Fund One Nationwide Plaza Box 1492 Columbus, Oh 43216 614/227-7559 800/848-0920 (toll-free)	M	500	PG	R	2,500	100	T, W

Class	Fund	AFF	MIN CK	SAF	YLD	INIT	ADD	EXP
P	Money Market Management, Inc. 421 Seventh Avenue Pittsburgh, PA 15219 412/288-1900 800/245-2442 (toll-free)	M	500	R	R	1,000	100	T, W
I	Money Market Trust 421 Seventh Avenue Pittsburgh, PA 15219 412/288-1900 800/245-2442 (toll-free)	M	NR	NR	NR	NR	NR	NR
P	Money Shares, Inc. One Wall Street New York, NY 10005 212/269-8800 800/221-5757 (toll-free)	M	1,000	NR	NR	1,000	100	T, W
P	MoneyMart Assets, Inc. 100 Gold Street New York, NY 10038 212/791-7123 800/221-7984 (toll-free)	B	500	R	G	1,000	500	T, W
P	Morgan Keegan Daily Cash Trust 421 Seventh Avenue Pittsburgh, PA 15219 412/288-1900 800/245-2442 (toll-free)	M	NR	NR	NR	5,000	1,000	NR
I	Mutual of Omaha Cash Reserve Fund, Inc. 3102 Farnam Street Omaha, NE 68131 402/342-3328 800/228-9011 (toll-free)	I	500	R	G	2,500	100	T, W
I	Mutual of Omaha Money Market Account, Inc. 3102 Farnam Street Omaha, NE 68131 402/342-3328 800/228-9011 (toll-free)	I	500	NR	NR	2,500	100	T, W
P	National Liquid Reserves, Inc. 605 Third Avenue New York, NY 10158 212/661-3000 800/223-7757 (toll-free) 212/661-3014 (collect)	B	$500	R	PG	$2,500	$100	T, W

Class	Fund	AFF	MIN CK	SAF	YLD	INIT	ADD	EXP
P	NEL Cash Management Trust 501 Boylston Street Boston, MA 02117 617/267-6600 800/225-7670 (toll-free)	I	250	R	G	1,000	0	T, W
P	NRTA-AARP U.S. Government Money Market Trust 421 Seventh Avenue Pittsburgh, PA 15219 412/288-1900 800/245-2442 (toll-free)	M	NR	G	X	500	100	NR
P	Oppenheimer Money Market Fund, Inc. Two Broadway New York, NY 10004 212/668-5100 800/221-9839 (toll-free)	B	500	X	G	2,500	100	T, W
P	Paine Webber CASHFUND, Inc. 140 Broadway New York, NY 10005 212/437-2121 800/221-5672 (toll-free)	B	500	PG	PG	5,000	500	T, W
P	Phoenix-Chase Money Market Fund One American Row Hartford, CT 06115 203/278-8050 800/343-2798 (toll-free)	M	NR	NR	NR	1,000	100	NR
P	Plimoney Fund, Inc. 111 North Broad Street Philadelphia, PA 19107 215/569-9300 800/523-4570 (toll-free)	I	NR	NR	NR	2,500	50	NR
P	Principal Protection Government Investment Fund, Inc. 327 S. LaSalle Street Chicago, IL 60604 312/939-5575 (collect)	M	NR	NR	NR	2,500	100	NR
P	Putnam Daily Dividend Trust One Post Office Square Boston, MA 02109 617/292-1000 800/225-1581 (toll-free)	M	500	R	G	2,000	500	T, W
P	Scudder Cash Investment Trust 175 Federal Street Boson, MA 02110 617/482-3990 800/225-2470 (toll-free)	M	500	R	G	1,000	0	T, W

Class Fund	AFF	MIN CK	SAF	YLD	INIT	ADD	EXP
P Security Cash Fund, Inc. 700 Harrison Street Topeka, KS 66636 913/295-3127 800/432-3536 (toll-free, KS only) 800/255-3509 (toll-free)	M	NR	NR	NR	1,000	100	NR
P Selected Money Market Fund, Inc. 6th Floor 111 West Washington Blvd. Chicago, Il 60602 312/630-2762 800/621-7321 (toll-free)	M	500	NR	NR	1,000	100	T, W
P Shearson Cash Government & Agencies Inc. 106th Floor Two World Trade Center New York, NY 10048 212/321-6554 800/221-7136 (toll-free from ME, VT, NH, MA, RI, CT, PA, NJ, DE) 800/221-2990 (toll-free, other states)	B	0	G	X	5,000	1,000	T, W
P Shearson Daily Dividend, Inc. 106th Floor Two World Trade Center New York, NY 10048 212/321-6554 800/221-7136 (toll-free from ME, VT, NH, MA, RI, CT, PA, NJ, DE) 800/221-2990 (toll-free, other states)	B	0	R	PG	5,000	1,000	T, W
P Short Term Income Fund, Inc. 230 Park Avenue New York, NY 10169 212/697-4570	M	500	PG	PG	1,000	100	T, W
P Sigma Government Securities Fund, Inc. Greenville Center 3801 Kennett Pike Wilmington, DE 19807 302/652-3091 800/441-9490 (toll-free)	M	NR	NR	NR	500	100	NR
P Sigma Money Market Fund, Inc. Greenville Center 3801 Kennett Pike Wilmington, DE 19807 302/652-3091 800/441-9490 (toll-free)	M	NR	NR	NR	500	100	NR

Class	Fund	AFF	MIN CK	SAF	YLD	INIT	ADD	EXP
P	St. Paul Money Fund, Inc. P.O. Box 43284 St. Paul, MN 55164 612/738-4271 800/328-1064 (toll-free)	M	500	X	G	3,000	500	T, W
P	SteinRoe Cash Reserves, Inc. 150 South Wacker Drive Chicago, IL 60606 312/368-7831 800/621-0615 (toll-free)	M	500	R	G	2,500	100	T, W
P	T. Rowe Price Prime Reserve 100 East Pratt Street Baltimore, Maryland 21202 301/547-2000 800/638-1527 (toll-free)	M	500	R	G	1,000	100	T, W
P	Texas Money Fund 6350 LBJ Freeway Suite 234 Dallas, TX 75240 214/239-3100	M	NR	NR	NR	2,000	0	NR
P	Transamerica Cash Reserve Box 2438 Terminal Annex Los Angeles, CA 90051 213/742-4141	M	500	R	PG	5,000	200	T, W
P	Trust for Cash Reserves 421 Seventh Avenue Pittsburgh, PA 15219 412/288-1900 800/245-2442 (toll-free)	B	0	R	R	5,000	500	T, W
I	Trust for Short-Term U.S. Government Securities 421 Seventh Avenue Pittsburgh, PA 15219 412/288-1900 800/245-2442 (toll-free)	M	NR	NR	NR	NR	NR	NR
I	Trust for U.S. Treasury Obligations 421 Seventh Avenue Pittsburgh, PA 15219 412/288-1900 800/245-2442 (toll-free)	M	NR	NR	NR	NR	NR	NR
P	Tucker Anthony Cash Management Fund Three Center Plaza Boston, MA 02108 617/523-3170 800/225-6258 (toll-free)	B	500	X	G	2,000	0	T, W

Class	Fund	AFF	MIN CK	SAF	YLD	INIT	ADD	EXP
P	Union Cash Management Fund, Inc. One Bankers Trust Plaza New York, NY 10006 212/432-4000 800/221-2450 (toll-free)	M	500	X	G	1,000	0	T, W
P	United Cash Management Fund, Inc. One Crown Center P.O. Box 1343 Kansas City, MO 64141 816/283-4000 800/821-5664 (toll-free)	M	500	X	G	1,000	100	T, W
P	USAA Money Market Fund Series 9800 Fredricksburg Rd. San Antonio, TX 78288 512/690-3390 800/531-8181 (toll-free)	M	NR	NR	NR	2,500	25	NR
P	Value Line Cash Fund, Inc. (The) 711 Third Avenue New York, NY 10017 212/687-3965 800/223-0818 (toll-free)	M	500	X	G	1,000	100	T, W
P	Vanguard Money Market Trust Federal Portfolio Prime Portfolio P.O. Box 876 Valley Forge, PA 19482 215/964-2600 800/523-7910 (toll-free)	M	500	X	G	3,000	100	T, W
P	Webster Cash Reserve Fund, Inc. 10 Hanover Square New York, NY 10005 212/747-3091	B	0	NR	NR	5,000	1,000	T, W

Appendix B

Growth of the Money Market Mutual Funds, 1975–1980

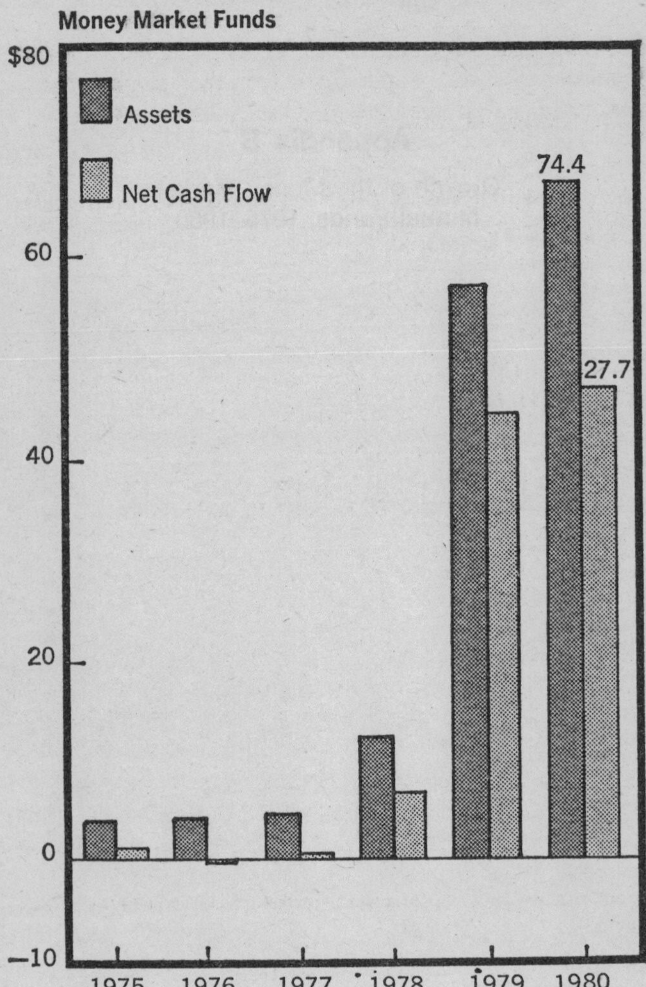

Source: 1981 Mutual Fund Factbook ICI. Money fund assets as of August 1, 1981, had increased to approximately $140 billion.

Money Fund Investment Motivation

The following is a condensation of the results of a questionnaire sent to people who inquired about money market funds from the Investment Company Institute.

People are interested in money market funds for somewhat different reasons. Please indicate the importance you attach to the following features. (Check more than one if appropriate).

Money market fund features	*Very important*		*Somewhat important*		*Not very important*	
	No. of respond.	*Percentage*	*No. of respond.*	*Percentage*	*No. of respond.*	*Percentage*
Money can be withdrawn at any time without penalty	1,239	77.0	328	20.4%	43	2.6
Small initial investment	901	59.0	498	32.6	129	8.4
No sales charge	1,044	68.7	427	26.1	48	3.2
No time requirement to earn maximum return	1,149	78.2	294	20.0	26	1.8
High current yield	1,562	96.2	57	3.5	4	0.3
Easy to add and withdraw money	1,132	73.9	359	23.5	40	2.6
Relatively safe	1,341	85.9	207	13.3	13	0.8
Free check writing	359	25.2	493	34.5	575	40.3
Telephone withdrawal	295	20.8	498	35.2	623	44.0
Daily declaration of dividends	509	36.0	508	35.9	398	28.1
Low expenses	924	65.5	418	29.6	69	4.9
Other	69	76.7	9	10.0	12	13.3

Have you purchased shares in a money market fund since you received the information from the Institute?

	Number of respondents	*Percent distribution*
Yes	821	48.6%
No	868	51.4
	1,689	100.0%

(continued)

Why did you purchase shares in a money market fund?

	Number of respondents	*Percent distribution*
High yield	606	78.7%
Ease of withdrawal	93	12.1
Reasonably safe	97	12.6
Low initial investments	38	4.9
Other	56	7.3
Refer to features in earlier question	95	12.3
Total	770	*
No response	919	

Do you regard your recent purchase of money market funds primarily as: (check one)

	Number of respondents	*Percent distribution*
Part of your longer-term savings program	416	51.4%
Way to achieve income, safety, and liquidity while awaiting improvements in stock or bond markets	171	21.1
Way to earn income for short period when temporary surplus of cash is available	193	23.9
Other	29	3.6
Total	809	100.0%
No Response	880	

SOURCE: 1981 Mutual Fund Fact Book. ICI.

Non-public Holdings of Money Funds, 1978–1980

Fiduciary, Business and Institutional Investors of Money Market Mutual Funds Value of Holdings, 1978 and 1980 (in thousands of dollars)

	1978	*1980*
FIDUCIARIES (BANKS AND INDIVIDUALS SERVING AS TRUSTEES, GUARDIANS AND ADMINISTRATORS) ..	$3,066,560	$15,427,717
Business corporations	609,760	6,974,270
Employee pension and profit-sharing funds ...	449,920	3,235,433

(continued)

	1978	1980
Insurance companies and other financial institutions	402,560	1,806,128
Unions	5,920	45,758
TOTAL BUSINESS ORGANIZATIONS	$1.468.160	$12.061.589
Churches and religious organizations	29,600	267,600
Fraternal, welfare, and other public associations	47,360	225,139
Hospitals, sanitariums, orphanages, etc	41,440	216,884
Schools and colleges	41,440	259,890
Foundations	—	19,708
TOTAL INSTITUTIONS AND FOUNDATIONS	$159,840	$989,221
OTHER INSTITUTIONAL INVESTORS NOT CLASSIFIED (a)	$1,225,440	$366,835
Total	$5,920,000	$28,845,362

(a) Includes institutional accounts which do not fall under other classifications and those for which no determination of classification can be made.

NOTE: Reporters of institutional data represented 92.9% of net assets in 1978 and 82.4% in 1980.

SOURCE: 1981 Mutual Fund Fact Book, ICI.

NOTE: At end of 1980, institutional investors held more than half of the money fund shares.

Non-public Number of Money Market Fund Accounts, 1978–1980

Fiduciary, Business and Institutional Investors of Money Market Funds Number of Accounts, 1978 and 1980

	1978	1980
FIDUCIARIES (BANKS AND INDIVIDUALS SERVING AS TRUSTEES, GUARDIANS AND ADMINISTRATORS)	79,742	402,824
Business corporations	13,036	187,235
Employee pension and profit-sharing funds	24,332	216,994
Insurance companies and other financial institutions	11,811	34,041
Unions	34	840
TOTAL BUSINESS ORGANIZATIONS	49,213	439,110

(continued)

	1978	*1980*
Churches and religious organizations	589	9,391
Fraternal, welfare and other public associations	454	6,158
Hospitals, sanitariums, orphanages, etc.......	411	3,884
Schools and colleges	404	4,763
Foundations	1	579
TOTAL INSTITUTIONS AND FOUNDATIONS	1,859	24,775
OTHER INSTITUTIONAL INVESTORS NOT CLASSIFIED (a)	15,315	18,884
Total	146,129	885,593

(a) Includes institutional accounts which do not fall under other classifications and those for which no determination of classification can be made.

NOTE: Reporters of institutional data represented 92.9% of net assets in 1978 and 82.4% in 1980.

•SOURCE: 1981 Mutual Fund Fact Book. ICI.

The Top Ten Money Market Banks in the United States

The Top Ten Money Market Banks in the United States

Bank	*1980 Assets $bn*	*1979 Total $bn*
Citicorp (New York)	114.92	71.771
BankAmerica (San Francisco)	111.617	88.426
Chase Manhattan (New York)	76.19	56.846
Manufacturers Hanover (New York)	55.522	41.745
Morgan J. P. (New York)	51.991	35.594
Continental Illinois (Chicago)	42.089	27.314
Chemical New York	41.342	30.067
Bankers Trust New York	34.202	23.816
Western Bankcorp. (Los Angeles)	32.11	24.864
First Chicago	28.699	21.361

SOURCE: The Financial Times (London). June 16, 1981.

Index